ADVANCE PRAISE FOR *WHIDBEY ISLAND*

"When you look carefully, the land speaks to you. You hear how people have chosen to care for it. This book tells the stories of Whidbey Island residents who never expected to become activists; but who saw harm to the land and were inspired to fight to conserve it."
—Estella Leopold, botanist, paleontologist, naturalist and professor emeritus of Biology at the University of Washington

"Who should read this book? Everyone who cares about conserving the land for future generations. This book tells the compelling stories of individuals who decided to make a difference. You can view Whidbey Island's history as a microcosm of successes and failures in land conservation."
—Christine Gregoire, governor, State of Washington, 2005–2013

"Whidbey Island: a microcosm in the Salish Sea. Land-use history here holds lessons from the past and present about the actions of individuals and the community to preserve and sustain the island's habitats and landscapes. These stories will inform and inspire readers, deepening our awareness of the paths other islanders have created for us to follow."
—Dyanne Sheldon, restoration ecologist

Whidbey Island

REFLECTIONS ON PEOPLE & THE LAND

ELIZABETH GUSS, JANICE O'MAHONY
& MARY RICHARDSON

Charleston London

THE
History
PRESS

Published by The History Press
Charleston, SC 29403
www.historypress.net

Copyright © 2014 by Elizabeth Guss, Janice O'Mahony and Mary Richardson
All rights reserved

Front cover: Ebey's Bluff in the Ebey's Landing National Historic Reserve. *Courtesy of
M. Denis Hill/Whidbey Panoramas.*
Back cover, left: Crocket Lake in the Ebey's Landing National Historic Reserve.
Courtesy of Mark Sheehan; *right*: Admiralty Inlet Natural Area Preserve in the Ebey's
Landing National Historic Reserve. *Courtesy of Mark Sheehan.*

First published 2014

Manufactured in the United States

ISBN 978.1.62619.277.5

Library of Congress CIP data applied for.

Contents

Harry and His Trees

On Glacier Peak along the Suiattle River Basin of Washington's North Cascade Mountains, teenager Harry Case walked through a ruined forest. It was an ugly, exploited landscape. Years later, he remembered those viciously clear-cut acres well: "They were so wasteful back then, it was just butchered. The pieces they left behind were so big you couldn't even climb over them. I was so disgusted by that logging. I was going to get my own place so no one would ever log it like that."

Harry put his plan into action in 1946 when he was only eighteen years old. He bought a 176-acre second-growth forest about three miles west of Langley on Whidbey Island for $840 in a tax foreclosure sale and got down to work.

For the next forty years, Harry went to his day job as a trombonist for the Seattle Symphony and raised his family. But whenever he found time, he tended his land. Painstakingly and quietly, he made his stand against the kind of destruction he had witnessed all those years ago in another once thriving forest. He taught himself how to sustain and manage his wooded acres, doing most of the work himself along with the help of his draft horse, Toby. He thinned trees to give others room to grow—removing dead, dying or deformed trees and planting hundreds of healthy new ones. In the process, he preserved animal habitat and wetlands. By 1956, he began selectively harvesting some of the trees so carefully and precisely that only he knows where all the stumps are.

After retiring from the symphony, he continued to work in the forest for twenty more years. Family and friends helped him tend a diverse, healthy

Harry Case, 2009. *Courtesy of Whidbey Camano Land Trust and Cheryl Lowe.*

and mature forest and to protect it from both ruinous logging and intense pressure from developers to turn it into thirty-five home sites. Today, it is brimming with Douglas fir, hemlock, alder and cedar, huckleberry, salal, mosses and ferns—the native flora typical of island conifer forests. It teems with animal and avian life, including hawks, owls, many species of birds, coyotes, deer, squirrels and rabbits. It is ecologically balanced, except for an overpopulation of deer resulting from a dearth of predators.

In the early 2000s, Harry began to learn from his grandson Shawn, long his helper in the forest, about the disastrous effects of carbon dioxide on Earth's atmosphere. Now with degrees in forestry and horticulture, Shawn knew some of this damage was clearly related to the destruction of the world's forests. Harry determined then to preserve his own small forest as a way of mitigating, however modestly, the devastating consequences of forest degradation.

In 2009, after sixty-four years of study, dedication and hard work, octogenarian Harry donated a conservation easement on his forest to the Whidbey Camano Land Trust. His community raised money to cover the project's cost, demonstrating its own commitment to these woods and its support for a neighbor who had tended the forest prudently for so many years. The trust is permanently protecting the property, now valued at more than $1.5 million, from clear cutting and development. And the thriving forest finally got an official name: Harry's Forest Forever.

Whidbey Island's history is full of stories like Harry's. Many generations of residents and visitors have responded to its unique environment. Newcomers quickly fall in love, and longtime residents stay passionately connected. If pressed, people will remark about the beauty of the two mountain ranges shining on the eastern and western horizons, the gentle climate, the winding country roads, the quick access to salt water from almost anywhere and the lakes, forest and open prairies. They may

Whidbey Islanders helping out with a work party at Harry's Forest Forever. *Courtesy of Whidbey Camano Land Trust.*

Whidbey Islanders and visitors rely on Washington State ferries. *Private collection.*

mention the peace, the relaxed pace of life and how their neighbors can be so friendly while they actively value individual privacy. They talk about the community's sophisticated arts and literary scenes, the local characters, the family-owned farms, the historic little towns and the bountiful marine resources. They tell of opportunities to make a fresh start or create a more graceful life. They describe how it feels to drive off the ferry and know that they have found their deepest and truest home.

On Whidbey Island as in many places, some earlier actions taken in ignorance or greed caused environmental devastation and cascading damage that haunt us today. But many islanders have discovered in themselves deep and often unexpected instincts to preserve and protect this beautiful but mistreated land— as Harry did in his forest.

This book shares some of these stories.

Acknowledgements

The authors sincerely thank all those who gave generously of time, memories, archives and pictures. There are so many of you, and each offered a perspective we couldn't have gained from any other source. We are also grateful to the authors whose writings about Whidbey—in books, pamphlets, news stories or websites—enriched our understanding of places and events.

We hope the stories we have written capture the rich and diverse culture of our beautiful island home.

All royalties from the sale of this book will be donated to the Whidbey Camano Land Trust.

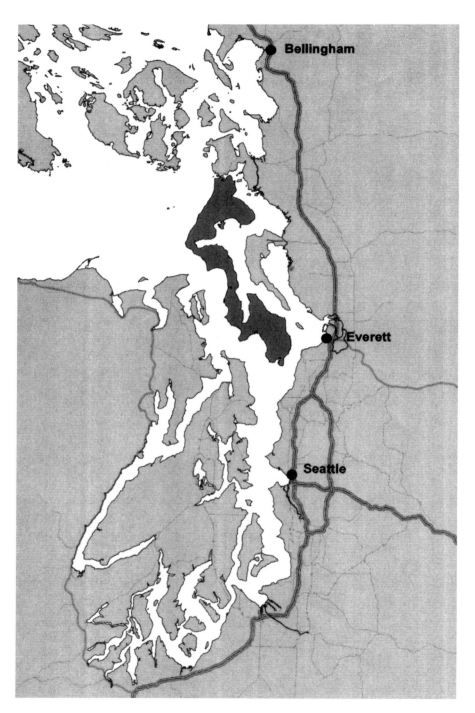

Whidbey Island's larger setting in Puget Sound. *Courtesy of Whidbey Camano Land Trust.*

One Island, Many Stories

The beauty and ineffable spirit of Whidbey Island engender deep feelings of connection and protectiveness in its people. For generations, its bounteous possibilities have inspired imaginations and motivated many variations of interaction between people and place.

This interchange is a common experience for Whidbey Islanders:

Where are you from?
Whidbey Island.
Oh, I love Whidbey!

Just as bonds between people have a variety of expression, so does the connection between people and place over time. Poet and writer Wendell Berry sums up this complex relationship:

It's mighty hard right now to think of anything that's precious that isn't endangered. There are no sacred and unsacred places; there are only sacred and desecrated places. My belief is that the world and our life in it are conditional gifts. We have the world to live in and the use of it on the condition that we will take good care of it. And to know it and to be willing to take care of it, we have to love it.

To live on Earth is to change it. We make many choices as we turn physical space into emotional place. We create a milieu in which to live and work,

Trees adapt to high winds on the bluff of Ebey's Prairie. *Courtesy of Whidbey Camano Land Trust.*

where we feel at home, safe and able to satisfy our basic needs. Thus, we are constantly modifying our natural environment, no matter how gently we try to walk upon the earth. Everyone leaves footprints. Even the decision to leave some land untouched requires the erection of physical or legal boundaries that become part of our collective landscape. All open spaces are bordered by fences of one kind or another, and the land thrives or withers under our feet based on the choices we make.

Each of us must discern our own sense of balance among issues such as land preservation, economic development, population growth, personal politics, habitat protection and what we consider to be essential to a healthy and sustainable environment. We always weigh a variety of options. Our community is then either nurtured or fractured by our choices and degree of consensus.

The environment itself responds to our choices by adaptation and change in habitat, animal and plant species, water quality and even topography. And we, in turn, make further adjustments to adapt to those new realities.

As the author Richard White states in his influential book *Land Use, Environment, and Social Change: The Shaping of Island County*:

The real history of the area is not political history, nor in a strict sense, social history, although it contains elements of each. Instead it is the history of changes wrought in the natural environment by both Indian and white occupation and use of the land, and the consequences of these changes for the people who made them.

As individuals, we study our past to achieve more of what we want and to stop repeating mistakes. Similarly, our best chance of ensuring a successful and healthy future comes when we understand the details of our past. What was happening then? What events were set in motion? What were the options for response? How did it all work out? What do people wish they had done differently? The answers to these questions shine a bright light on the road forward. When we learn from the experiences of those who came before us, we gain invaluable tools and powerful clues to help us master civic problems and maximize opportunities for the common good.

Whidbey Island 101

It is metaphoric of Whidbey Island culture that people offer varying opinions about its most basic characteristics. There is no agreement on its exact size. Distances on the island seem oddly malleable. On the main highway, a directional sign in the town of Coupeville states, "Oak Harbor 10 Miles," and going the other way, a sign in Oak Harbor states "Coupeville 8 Miles."

Some say that's because it's downhill going to Coupeville.

As of this writing, neither the Island County Public Works Department nor the Planning & Community Development Department could give an exact measurement. But everyone acknowledges the island is long and narrow. It is said to be thirty-five to fifty-eight miles long, depending on how one measures the curving distance between Deception Pass at the far north end and Cultus Bay at the south. It is variously described as ten to twelve miles across at its widest point and one or two miles at its narrowest. It may be impossible to know Whidbey Island's exact dimensions because its size is constantly being changed by tidal soil accretion or erosion.

To the west are the bluffs of Admiralty Inlet of Puget Sound and the Strait of Juan de Fuca. To the east are the calmer waters of Possession Sound and Saratoga Passage. Estimates of the island's area range from 169 to 235 square miles, depending on the source consulted. The island has from 148 to 200 miles of shoreline—again, depending on the source. We do know that Whidbey Island has forests at both ends and open prairies and farmlands in the middle.

Island County Historical Society Museum director Richard Castellano says that "nobody seems to know" the length, breadth or area of Whidbey Island. He says it has been an ongoing discussion, particularly when there is the periodic dust-up over whether Whidbey Island or New York's Long Island is the longest island in the contiguous lower forty-eight states. This argument continues to simmer, occasionally breaking out into open discord, despite a 1985 Supreme Court decision that declared Long Island to be a peninsula and the existence of other contenders for the title of "longest" such as 113-mile-long Padre Island in Texas.

Whidbey Island sits in the northern half of Puget Sound about thirty miles north of Seattle, partly in the rain shadow of the Olympic Mountain Range to the west. Other than by private vessel, there are only three ways off the island. One can drive off over the beautiful two-span Deception Pass Bridge (completed in 1935) at the north end, continuing over Fidalgo Island onto the mainland. One can take a twenty-minute ferry ride onto the mainland at the south end, arriving at Mukilteo, a small city abutting the larger city of Everett. Or one can go to the middle of the island, near Coupeville, from which a thirty-five minute ferry ride connects Whidbey Island with the historic little city of Port Townsend on the Olympic Peninsula. That's it.

Sunset over Deception Pass, one of many scenic vistas. *Private collection.*

Iconic tree at top of Ebey's Bluff. *Courtesy of Whidbey Camano Land Trust and photographer Mark Sheehan.*

Whidbey is only a mile and a half across the Saratoga Passage from Camano Island, the second-largest island in Washington's Island County. But you can't get there from here. You have to drive off Whidbey Island by ferry or bridge, and the shortest route by car between the sister islands takes more than an hour and a half.

The driving distance between the two islands compared to the distance by water illustrates very well why settlers relied on water transportation even after some roads were built. People and goods moved quickly by water. Soon after whites began to settle Whidbey Island, there were frequent steamers from Seattle to the Whidbey Island communities of Langley, Coupeville and Oak Harbor as well as regular mail delivery and direct access to Seattle, Tacoma and the state capital of Olympia. Public transportation onto and off the island came early. In 1913, a ferry service started across Deception Pass, linking the island to the mainland. In the 1920s, the ferry service began taking passengers off the south end and middle part of the island.

As cars replaced canoes and steamers, travel became more difficult. People chose to bump along on rough, narrow roads rather than glide easily and quickly through the water. Islanders became more psychologically isolated from the mainland, and that sense of isolation continues today in both positive and negative ways.

It's one of the paradoxes of living on Whidbey that a short trip across the water becomes more momentous than it really is. Every Whidbey Islander has experienced the sense of peaceful separation from traffic and stress that comes with the short ferry ride out of congested and chaotic urban environments. And most Whidbey Islanders have experienced the unexpected all-day social event, when mainland friends invited over for a visit settle in for the whole day, feeling they have traveled so far and are facing such an arduous journey back.

A Quiet Place

Of Whidbey Island's 58,000 residents, most live in rural areas. Oak Harbor, the largest Whidbey Island city, has a population of 22,075 people. The two other small cities on the island are the county seat of Coupeville (population 1,831) and Langley (population 1,065). Among several unincorporated communities are Greenbank (population 1,837) and Clinton (population 928.)

The Whidbey Naval Air Station, three miles outside Oak Harbor, is the major economic driver for the north end of the island. About 7,600 military and 2,400 civilians work there. The remainder of the island's brick-and-mortar economy relies on tourism, agriculture and the arts. Increasingly, Internet-based businesses are springing up. Whidbey is attractive to entrepreneurs who conduct their work online in fields such as communications, consultation, marketing, graphic design and website development.

By the 1900s, Whidbey Island was already a popular destination for vacationers and tourists, especially in the summer—and that custom continues to this day. Ferry line brochures promoted "Romantic Whidbey Island" as a place for tourism, summer homes, vacation cabins and resorts.

In common with residents of many communities that experience regular infusions of tourists, Whidbey Islanders are grateful for the economic benefits of tourism but are occasionally irritated by increased traffic and "off-islanders" who don't understand how to queue for ferries or that they should always pull off the road for emergency vehicles and never rudely overtake other cars on the highway. And don't get them started on the "two- or three-boat waits" in the ferry lines on nice Sunday afternoons when the vacationers pack up to go back to their cities on the mainland, variously described by islanders as "the other side," "over town," "overseas" or "America."

SETTLEMENT

Whidbey Island has always been a place of sparse population but active human involvement. Native American interaction with the island dates from the last ice age fourteen thousand years ago. Human habitation is found in the archaeological record from ten to twelve thousand years ago. There were waves of settlement by the native peoples of various tribal races and cultures, but by 1300, the region was inhabited and controlled by the Salish peoples. Two tribes from this group, the Snohomish and the Skagit, became the primary residents of Whidbey Island, the former in the south and the latter in the north.

The indigenous people lived in what is called "seasonal rounds": they moved from sheltered winter villages to spring root camps, summer fishing camps and fall hunting camps. They also used specialized sites for particular activities such as logging, bark-stripping and quarrying rock. Sacred sites were characterized by pictographs or petroglyphs. Burial sites were of great spiritual meaning as well.

The Salish on the island were decimated by diseases brought by white contact in the eighteenth century, only to be quickly physically displaced by white settlers in the nineteenth century. Not only did white settlers appropriate Whidbey lands for themselves, but their farming and animal husbandry practices also destroyed the hunting, gathering and agricultural processes that had sustained the native people for generations.

The Treaty of Point Elliott (1855) represented the formal ceding of what had been Salish lands to white hegemony after generations of destruction of the native peoples' way of life. By the early 1900s, most of Whidbey's native people had relocated to a reservation that the treaty created near La Conner.

White settlers began arriving on Whidbey Island as part of the epic westward movement of the mid-1800s. The first white farmer arrived in 1850. The island's economy quickly diverged, as new settlers chose farming, fishing or logging to build their new lives.

A wave of Irish immigrants settled on Whidbey during the diaspora associated with the potato famine of the mid-1800s. By the 1890s, Dutch immigrants began to come in significant numbers. To this day, the people of Oak Harbor enthusiastically celebrate their Irish and Dutch heritages with the annual St. Patrick's Day parade and Holland Happening festival.

Scandinavians began arriving in large numbers around 1900. By 1920, they composed a fifth of the island's population but nearly half of its farming families.

In the 1870s, a small but significant Chinese population began to arrive on the island after working elsewhere as transcontinental railroad or mine workers. By 1880, the Chinese represented 45 percent of the farm laborers in the county. By 1900, many had become tenant farmers, primarily growing potatoes. In the 1900 census, they were counted as being 28 percent of land renters and sharecroppers. They were very successful farmers, initially appreciated by the white farmers because of their productivity, their care for the land and the fact that they paid more than other tenants to rent the land. The Chinese population peaked at seventy-six in 1890 but then began to decline due to anti-Chinese agitation and xenophobia. By 1900, white vigilantes, fueled by accusations that the Chinese were somehow responsible for the economic depression that had recently affected the entire region, succeeded in driving the Chinese farmers out with intimidation and slander. By 1920, only eight Chinese were listed in the census. Some of the fear-based rhetoric of the time of Chinese expulsion is eerily echoed in today's immigration debates: they're taking jobs from white Americans, they're sending all their money out of the country, they don't assimilate and they are here illegally.

By the 1930s, foreign immigration to Whidbey Island had virtually ceased, to be replaced by the poor and displaced from urban areas of Washington and other parts of the United States. Two waves of farmers arrived. Some moved because of the effects of the longstanding drought on the northern plains. People fleeing the Dust Bowl began to arrive in the early 1930s. Desperate to find a place to support their families, these people often lacked the capital or skills to be successful, especially since by then, much of the available farmland was infertile, depleted and ravaged by logging. But as Richard White states, "The worse the land, the greater its availability and the greater the influx of immigrants."

During World War II, new people arrived to build and staff the Whidbey Naval Air Station. In the late 1960s and '70s, children of the counterculture began to arrive for the fresh start Whidbey Island has always offered to newcomers. From the '50s through the '70s, many "summer" families began to convert their small beach cabins to year-round residences to live

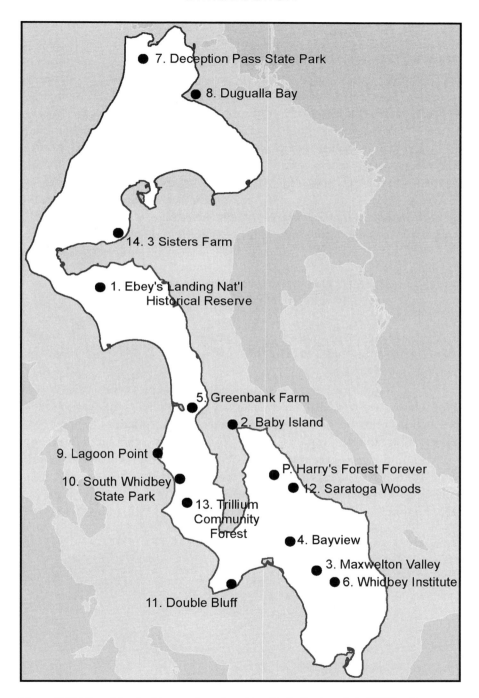

7. Deception Pass State Park

8. Dugualla Bay

14. 3 Sisters Farm

1. Ebey's Landing Nat'l Historical Reserve

5. Greenbank Farm

2. Baby Island

9. Lagoon Point

P. Harry's Forest Forever

10. South Whidbey State Park

12. Saratoga Woods

13. Trillium Community Forest

4. Bayview

3. Maxwelton Valley

6. Whidbey Institute

11. Double Bluff

Map of Whidbey Island with story locations identified. *Courtesy of the Whidbey Camano Land Trust.*

in during retirement. Despite these conversions, second homes still make up a significant portion of Whidbey Island properties. Financial conditions of the '80s and '90s drew an increase in people from urban areas—Seattle, its suburban cities and California—attracted by a thriving real estate market and easy credit. Industry in Everett and Seattle has always made Whidbey attractive to hardy commuters. As always, artists, writers and musicians arrived, drawn to the spirit of place. Now, in the first decades of the twenty-first century, new generations of farmers and Internet entrepreneurs add richness and diversity to the mix.

The question, "How did you happen to come to Whidbey?" is usually the first one asked among recent arrivals, and everyone has a story. Usually the story is a love story—love of the spirit of place and the vibrant community.

LET US SHOW YOU AROUND!

In the following pages we will visit fourteen special places on Whidbey Island. Each place holds part of the story of how people have interacted with the land over time.

Every change in the land has changed us as a community. Every story illustrates some aspect of the complexity of human settlement, development, population growth, political power, scientific knowledge, repurposing, preservation and restoration. In this complicated interaction, we come together, and we are bitterly divided. We have made irrevocable decisions, some of which make us proud and some which we wish we had done differently. We find ourselves in a continual process of learning from our past, hoping to become wiser stewards of our place in the future.

1

Ebey's Landing National Historical Reserve

The iconic center of Whidbey has beckoned and provided for people for centuries. When development threatened rich farmland and a way of life, citizens joined together to find a way to protect the place and care for their home. The outcome has shaped a new way of thinking about interweaving history and contemporary life.

NOVEMBER 10, 1978, WAS an extraordinary moment in time. That day, President Jimmy Carter signed Public Law 95-625, which created the first—and still only—such reserve in the country. Against formidable odds, an eight-year effort by local farmers and the larger community to save farmland and natural areas had birthed a new kind of national park, one intended to honor and protect a remarkable cultural landscape. Like all newly born conservation projects, the reserve had context from the past and a future to discover.

A unit of the National Park Service, the Ebey's Landing National Historical Reserve was unique in many ways from the start. Instead of honoring one specific historic time period, Congress recognized the reserve for its significance in the "unbroken historical record of the Central Whidbey community in Puget Sound from the nineteenth century explorations and settlement to the present time." It came to be managed by an innovative public-private partnership. Private property owners could choose whether to protect their land.

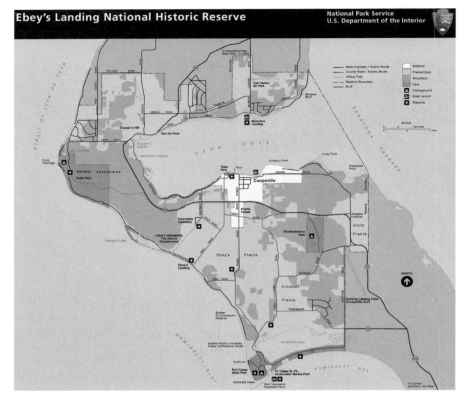

Map of Ebey's Landing. *Courtesy of the National Park Service.*

LIVING HISTORY PANORAMA

At the Ebey's Overlook near Sunnyside Cemetery in the reserve, you view a living cultural landscape. On all sides is evidence of the interrelationship of people and the land, how they have influenced each other over time. Layered into the soil, the plants, the buildings and the roads, the landscape holds a long and diverse cultural history. Straight ahead is the colorful mosaic of many small farms, large squares of loamy brown soil alternating with orderly stripes of crops. Edging them are clusters of trees, small forests that give texture and height and contrast with cultivated fields.

To the right is the Admiralty Inlet, a saltwater gateway to the Pacific Ocean. At its edge is the iconic Ebey's Bluff, beloved of hikers, artists and wildlife. Farther down the coast are the remnants of Fort Casey Military Reservation, now a state park, historic museum and conference center.

Crockett Lake. *Courtesy of Whidbey Camano Land Trust and photographer Mark Sheehan.*

Beyond that is Crockett Lake, a precious spot along the North American Flyway and an Audubon Important Birding Area.

Hidden behind tall trees to the left is the historic town of Coupeville, one of Washington State's oldest incorporated cities and the Island County seat. The Coupeville dock juts out into the waters of Penn Cove, an exceptional U-shaped inlet rich with marine life, beaches and memories. The fragrance of salt water, the breeze that rustles through leaves, the calls of eagles, hawks and crows and even the traffic light create a postcard of remarkable Central Whidbey.

Beautiful, colorful and expansively alive, the reserve incorporates its history in daily life while its management and residents grapple with issues that affect its future. Ebey's 17,400 acres host working farms, vibrant culture, state parks and a variety of nationally acclaimed attributes and festivals. Nearly half is open space and agricultural, more than a third is woodlands and some 5 percent is wetlands. The remaining area is residential and urban-commercial. Restoration efforts underway in the reserve focus on native prairies and historic buildings as well as finding new uses for historic military facilities. History and contemporary life together generate enthusiasm and a desire to care for this place for future generations.

Understanding the reserve begins with the land. This diverse, rich ecosystem has always attracted people who both changed the land and were

A view of Mount Rainier. *Courtesy of Whidbey Camano Land Trust.*

changed by it. The reserve is maturing in a complex ecological, historical, cultural and economic matrix.

Composed of debris left by receding glaciers, Whidbey Island came into being some fourteen thousand years ago. The reserve spans a narrow bend in the north-central part of the island, a section where no place is farther than a couple of miles from shore. The centerpiece of the reserve is Ebey's Prairie, a broad, trough-shaped lowland, originally a glacial lake and subsequently very productive agricultural land. With its generally mild, marine climate, Central Whidbey has hosted over millennia many species of flora and fauna—some native, some introduced, some eliminated by human activity and some invaders that have spread aggressively and choked out gentler species.

The first human inhabitants of this area were native tribes. Since the fourteenth century, they had been the Skagit people, part of the Coast Salish tribes who migrated seasonally, following salmon runs and gathering wild plants. In their regular seasonal dwelling areas, these communities helped maintain prairies for centuries. They burned back the encroaching forests, creating open space for hunting and some agriculture. The tribes planted dietary staples, most notably camas and bracken fern. What they grew changed as white settlers introduced new plants. Turns out the prairies grew pretty good potatoes, too.

The historical significance of the reserve is elegantly summarized in the legislation that created it. The document referred specifically to four historic eras: Vancouver's exploration of the Puget Sound in 1792, the first permanent settlement on Whidbey Island led by Isaac Ebey, the Donation Land Claim settlement and subsequent settlements and the development of the historic town of Coupeville. These areas illustrate, on a very local level, some of the major themes playing out then in North America.

VANCOUVER'S EXPLORATION OF PUGET SOUND

Since its discovery by Europeans in the late fifteenth century, the American continent had been a theater where rival European empires competed to expand trade and political reach. Occasional expeditions along the Pacific Coast began in the sixteenth century, and systematic exploration started in the 1770s.

Captain George Vancouver and the crew of *Discovery*, flying the British flag, entered the Strait of Juan de Fuca in the spring of 1792. They explored, charted and then named the lands they encountered. Vancouver named the Sound for his lieutenant, Peter Puget, and Whidbey Island for the ship's master, Joseph Whidbey, who sailed around and mapped the island. Shortly thereafter, four empires—Spain, Russia, Britain and America—vied for control of trade in the northwestern territory. Enterprising individuals bartered tools, manufactured goods and some foods for fur. This vibrant interchange between whites and native people continued for decades.

Settlers also came across the United States by land and established homesteads in the Puget Sound area. As the fur trade began to slow and more Americans settled the land, British interest in the area waned. The 1846 Treaty of Oregon resolved the political conflict over who would control and govern the area after Britain agreed to settle the international boundary at the forty-ninth parallel. Whidbey Island would be a U.S. territory.

FIRST PERMANENT SETTLEMENT

Just two years later, active Euro-American settlement of Whidbey Island began. Thomas Glasgow briefly established a farm on what is today known as Ebey's Prairie. Then came Samuel Crockett, who was initially lured west by the California gold rush but who soon traveled north to explore possibilities in Puget Sound. He sent glowing reports about the Whidbey prairie to family and friends, including to a close friend in Missouri, Isaac Neff Ebey. In 1850, Ebey took advantage of a U.S. government incentive to entice people to relocate to the Oregon Territory (covering modern-day Oregon, Washington and Idaho). He traveled to Central Whidbey and claimed for himself and his wife, Rebecca, a complete section, a full square mile of the prairie that today bears his name. He is considered the first permanent Euro-American settler on Whidbey Island.

Enterprising, industrious and with a strong sense of community obligation, Isaac Ebey quickly distinguished himself. Besides planting crops, Ebey built a dock on his beach for commercial traffic, especially trade from Port Townsend. He played key roles in early territorial affairs as prosecuting attorney for the Whidbey Island community and representative to the Oregon Territorial legislature.

Ebey helped secure the separation of Washington from the Oregon Territory in 1853, was instrumental in establishing Island County in 1853 (the eighth county in the Washington Territory) and became customs officer in Port Townsend, the official port of entry for Puget Sound. During the mainland Indian Wars of 1855–56, he raised a company of volunteers whom he led in battle, earning the title colonel. Rebecca and the Ebeys' two young sons joined him in 1852. Already weak from tuberculosis, Rebecca died a year later following the birth of their daughter. Ebey himself died suddenly and violently in 1857, killed by warrior Indians from Canada who sought revenge for the death of one of their chiefs (*tyee*) the prior year. Ebey was considered an important enough "chief" that his death was sufficient to avenge the insult. No one else in the family was harmed.

Donation Land Claim Act

Ebey had responded to an incentive known as the Oregon Donation Land Claim Act of 1850, a forerunner of the Homestead Act. Passed by Congress to encourage people to settle the far territories, the act granted large parcels of land to those who arrived before December 1, 1850. A married couple could claim a full section, 640 acres. A single man could claim 320 acres, and if he married in the next year, his wife could claim another 320 acres in her own name. No purchase was needed, just the requirement to build a home and live there, cultivating at least 5 acres for four years to own it outright. The act was extended to offer half the acreage to later claimants. By 1855, when the act expired, some twenty-nine settlers to Central Whidbey Island had established holdings.

TOWN OF COUPEVILLE

Over the next few decades, more settlers came to central Whidbey to farm, fish and become business people. Outside the prairie, people carved farms out of forests or on reclaimed marshland. Along Penn Cove, they established towns and villages. Coveland (where the community of San de Fuca is today) was the site of the original county seat and principal trading center for Whidbey. But by the 1870s, it was overshadowed by Coupeville, the town named for Captain Thomas Coupe and built on the acreage of his Donation Land claim. Coupeville, on the south side of the wonderful, natural harbor of Penn Cove, was more convenient for farmers and merchants than Coveland, and it became the county seat in 1881. Many of the oldest still-standing homes in Washington State were built in the larger Coupeville area, holding some of the historical significance that the reserve honors in architecture. Coupeville was finally incorporated in 1910.

This land appealed to many enterprising souls. There were two brief but notable speculative frenzies on Whidbey Island, fueled by the false hopes of a railroad coming through. In the late 1860s, hotels were built in Coupeville amid rumors that the Northern Pacific Railroad would build a terminus at Coupeville. Twenty years later, another rumor put a railroad terminus in Port Townsend. That sparked platting of town sites—called Chicago and Brooklyn—along the Keystone Spit across the Admiralty Inlet from Port Townsend. In the late 1890s, as the U.S. Army built Fort Casey on the Admiralty Inlet, workers briefly inhabited Chicago and Brooklyn. Keystone Spit would come into the public spotlight again decades later as a movement to protect open space for the public gained momentum.

COST OF GROWTH

While the Donation Land Claim Act certainly encouraged white settlement, it completely ignored the native people who had made central Whidbey Island their home for centuries. Some historical sources claim that Washington Territorial governor Isaac Stevens made oral promises to the native people about their lands that were contradicted by the written treaties that tribal leaders signed. Whites received titles to land historically used by the tribes. Many native people left Whidbey within a few years of the 1855 Treaty of Point Elliott.

Also during the early years of settlement, new farmers on Whidbey became concerned about the native predator species and their killing of livestock. Farmers systematically trapped and killed bears, large cats and wolves. To trap the wolves, farmers laced carcasses with strychnine. In less than a decade, all wolves were gone. The triumph of humans over nature seemed inevitable, though not without consequence. Even today, indiscriminate killing of coyotes continues in parts of Whidbey. This historic disregard of wildlife's importance in a healthy ecosystem would eventually clash with an emerging consciousness that respected nature and its complex systems as much or more than family tradition or economic gain.

A spectacular collision occurred in the waters of Penn Cove in the early 1970s. The U-shaped inlet in Central Whidbey is abundant with marine life and the location of many residents' childhood memories of happy summer times playing in the water and on the beach. Penn Cove twice became the corral for orcas herded in for capture. Major marine park owners were eager to purchase young orcas and train them for shows in the increasingly popular marine parks. During 1970–71, ten young orcas were stolen from their families at Penn Cove. Those who had enjoyed the exciting spectacle of dozens of orcas at close range watched the theft and brutality in horror. Jean Sherman, a Coupeville resident since the 1930s, recalls how people heard the orcas cry as family members were taken away, and the witnesses then wept themselves. Some orcas were killed and their bodies weighted down so that they would sink to the cove floor. When those bodies washed up on shore a few months later, people were outraged.

When the herding of orcas began again a year later, Don McGaffin, a Seattle reporter vacationing on Whidbey, moved quickly to film the capture. His coverage led to a public outcry that resulted in ending the orca abduction early. The Penn Cove captures were two of dozens from

1965 to 1976. Washington State outlawed captures for marine parks in 1976 in part due to the sustained protest following the Penn Cove captures. The resident orca populations in Puget Sound have yet to recover from the loss of so many young.

THE COMMUNITY RALLIES

During this time, Whidbey Island's population increased, and Island County commissioners showed a strong pro–growth and development preference. In response, a growing movement began to protect the beautiful and distinctive area around Coupeville. It is the opening chapter of the establishment of the reserve.

As author Laura McKinley explains in her rich 1993 account of this community effort, *Administrative History of Ebey's Landing National Historical Reserve*:

> *The story began simply enough with one family's decision in 1970 to rezone a portion of their farm. Little in the history of Whidbey Island to that point had suggested that a quiet request to the Island County Board of Commissioners would trigger a prolonged dispute among citizens of central Whidbey Island. In fact, the controversy that erupted would require more than a decade to resolve. Once the dust settled, the farm remained intact and the local residents had achieved a unique partnership with the National Park Service and local government. Not surprisingly in a small community whose roots are deeply entwined, some bitter feelings lingered. Even within the Ebey's Landing National Historical Reserve, the future state of the landscape is by no means assured.*

Since 1917, the Smith family had owned about half the original Ebey claim. By the late 1960s, the two Smith brothers realized that their farms were not profitable and they wanted to develop part of their land. Their initial request to rezone 82 acres was granted, and a year later, they made a second request for an additional 124 acres.

Some neighbors were alarmed about the threat to one of the prime open spaces on the island and the certain loss of farmland. Others felt development in open spaces to be quite necessary and inevitable. They resented efforts to obstruct what they saw as progress. Many attended a public hearing on the Smiths' 124-acre request. Probably no one wanted the prairie rezoned for residential development, but the Smiths were seriously in debt; farming was not a profitable venture for them. The county commissioners approved the rezone request. In just a few months, to complicate the situation, Knight Smith died suddenly and his widow, Roberta, faced inheritance taxes.

The story continued, folding back on itself multiple times with controversy, conflicts of interest for government officials, development plans and loans and foreclosures. Developers working on plans for the prairie were distracted by exciting, speculative efforts on the Keystone Spit. The zigzag pattern of activities, delays and efforts was dizzying; all the while, local people continued to make a living and simultaneously learn how to effect change in government policies. Federal and state elected officials recognized the critical importance of protecting the prairie and the spectacular view for public benefit. Local farmers knew that if land were subdivided and houses built, it would be the end of farming on this very productive soil.

The Keystone Spit, earlier the site of the speculative towns of Chicago and Brooklyn, once again appealed to private developers seeking fortunes in waterfront housing developments. New residents, including Al and Maurine Ryan, undertook the enormous challenge of stopping the privatization of the beach. Their goal became their organization's name—Saving Whidbey Island for Tomorrow (SWIFT). They persevered to ensure that the public maintained beach access and beautiful vistas along Crockett Lake.

Barley field in the Ebey's Reserve. *Courtesy of Whidbey Camano Land Trust.*

Across Central Whidbey, neighbors were repeatedly challenged to face and resolve, in healthy ways, significant differences of opinion. They faced broad questions: What did they value most in their home and environment? What actions would they take to protect what they valued? Those years of effort led to a growing sophistication about grass-roots efforts to hold local government officials accountable. Many formal legal actions were filed. Finally, the unfolding of the story led to innovative legislation at federal and state levels.

ANCILLARY BENEFITS

Along the way to securing President Carter's signature, the Ebey residents' efforts resulted in several significant accomplishments. Jimmie Jean Cook of Coupeville undertook a complete inventory of historic buildings. She found that Coupeville had the greatest number still standing in any Puget Sound community. Her work led to recognition of Coupeville in 1973 as a historic district in the National Register of Historic Places. It was the largest one in the country at that time.

Conifer seed orchard in Ebey's Landing, a new type of agriculture. *Courtesy of Whidbey Camano Land Trust.*

The first local land conservancy on Whidbey Island was established to hold conservation easements. The Ebey's Landing Open Space Foundation (ELOSF) sought funds to help purchase the conservation easements from the (now) two Smith widows. These funds would both help protect the land and alleviate the women's grievous financial difficulties in the late 1970s. The ELOSF's work and holding of conservation easements led quite directly to the establishment of the Whidbey Camano Land Trust in 1984.

Locals studied England's Greenline Parks—known for a mix of public-private ownership and intergovernmental cooperation and partnerships—as a possible model for a way to protect the land. In 1976 the National Park Service defined the national reserve concept to meet the growing need of rural communities to protect resources for public benefit. The reserve concept depended heavily on a partnership approach to governance. In the Ebey's Reserve, the trust board—composed of representatives of the National Park Service, Island County, Washington State Parks and the town of Coupeville—became the governing entity.

Quite notably, from this significant effort emerged a growing consciousness about the need for local, community action to protect Whidbey Island's natural heritage for the benefit of all. A new spirit was taking shape about the relationship of people and the land.

Why the Reserve Matters

The eight-year effort to create the reserve is rich with human interest and high drama. It showcases behavior across the spectrum: from the generosity and nobility of many through desperate decisions by some to misguided and opportunistic priorities of others. In 1993, the National Park Service published Laura McKinley's account of the achievement, complete with descriptions of how U.S. representative Lloyd Meeds and Senator Henry Jackson assembled bipartisan support to include Ebey's in the comprehensive National Parks and Recreation Act of 1978.

There remain many open questions concerning the reserve. They cover a wide spectrum. What is the long-term role of the National Park Service? How effective are voluntary conservation easements to maintain the character of the landscape? What is and will continue to be the impact of increased visitors? How can we effectively manage the tension between public and private rights? Most of the land in the reserve was and is privately

Walking trail in Ebey's Reserve along the famous Ebey's Bluff. *Courtesy of Whidbey Camano Land Trust.*

owned. Within zoning limits, private property owners can still develop their lands—and what will that mean for the reserve?

The answers to these questions continue to unfold. In the years since the reserve was established, people still actively strive to care for this treasure. For years, the Whidbey Camano Land Trust has worked with property owners there to protect their farmland with conservation easements. People continue to restore historic buildings. An endangered prairie plant species, the Golden Paintbrush, has been found on a few sites in the reserve, and significant efforts are underway to restore it to a vibrant population. That requires restoring the prairie, a long-term process involving many scientific disciplines and much perseverance. The reserve itself draws visitors from around the world who then learn about Whidbey Island, its history and its culture. As the reserve marks its anniversary every November, we celebrate the vision and determination to keep that beautiful, productive cultural landscape a treasure for present and future generations to experience.

Still the only historical reserve in the country, it reflects a different way of thinking. As National Park Service historian Gretchen Luxenberg explained in 2013, the reserve "was the place that helped the National Park Service understand, at a landscape level, the importance of context... the land/environment in which resources and activities have occurred. Ebey's changed how the Park Service looked at cultural resources by

The endangered Golden Paintbrush is recovering through diligent restoration efforts of conservationists. *Courtesy of Whidbey Camano Land Trust and Mark Sheehan photographer.*

including cultural landscapes as a type of resource, and Ebey's was the guinea pig."

For centuries, this land fostered life and connection with nature. It became the canvas on which successive societies painted their lives and expressed their deep values. The stunning Ebey's Bluff is the iconic image of Whidbey Island to millions. In the story of how this place and its residents shaped one another, we see determination, cooperation and a vibrant, living relationship. In learning of the heroic effort to protect farmland and lifestyle, we touch permanence and stability, qualities rare in our change-addicted society.

2
Baby Island

Rising seas and shifting sands threaten a dot of land left from the glacier age. Both native tribes and white settlers enjoyed Baby Island, which was developed into a fishing resort in the early twentieth century. Today, the Tulalip tribes own the unpopulated island and still hope to stem its erosion.

FADING SKIES CAST HUES of red, yellow and orange as night falls. It's a dramatic backdrop for Baby Island—a brilliant canvas of dark, lacey patterns formed by the shape of sparse limbs—all that remain of the trees and shrubs that once sat atop this speck of ground. The island, formed some fourteen thousand years ago by receding glaciers, is in its sunset period. Once more than an acre in size, it now measures barely 80 by 230 feet at high tide and is gradually shrinking as wind and tides take their toll, aided by a rising sea level. It is a reminder that nature is the ultimate designer.

Baby Island—called Hackney Island on marine charts—sits at the confluence of Saratoga Passage and Holmes Harbor, a large, sheltered bay in the south part of Whidbey Island. Holmes Harbor was originally named "inside the bay" by the Snohomish tribal people—*sdukalbix*, or "People of the Moon"—who made South Whidbey Island their home from about AD 1200.

For centuries, the Snohomish people camped, clammed and fished on Baby Island. When they relinquished their island lands as part of the Treaty of Point Elliott in 1855, this special place remained an important part of Snohomish tribal history. It is a heritage site, a spiritual and ancestral home.

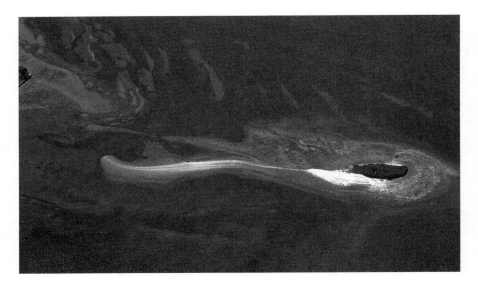

Baby Island, 1990. The tip of Rocky Point can be seen to the left. The view is toward Holmes Harbor. Saratoga Passage is to the left of the Island. *Courtesy of Washington State Department of Ecology.*

Starfish among the clamshells. *Private collection.*

Just 1,300 feet of Holmes Harbor seabed separate Baby Island from Whidbey Island. Yet this short distance is impassable except by boat unless there is an exceptionally low tide, called a minus low tide. Tidal waters can rise and fall from a minus-3.5-foot low in summer to a 15-foot high in the winter.

When a minus low tide does occur, usually during a full or new moon, beachcombers cross the short distance to Baby Island from Whidbey's Saratoga Beach, a stretch of sand that fronts Holmes Harbor. They pick their way among rocks, shells, eelgrass and tide pools, stepping gingerly to avoid the patches of sandal-eating muck scattered across the exposed tide flats.

Along the path, red, orange and purple starfish hug rocks covered with the barnacles they feed on. Clam spurts shoot up from the beds below. A shelf made from sand, crushed barnacles and clamshells sits like a runway to the rocky top of Baby Island, where a few scrub trees stand, all that can be seen when the tide is high.

Remnants of a pier and what were once concrete foundations hint of the fishing camp whose buildings dwarfed the small island during the middle years of the twentieth century. Little evidence remains of the Snohomish tribal people and the hundreds of years they made camp here.

Land of Our Ancestors

The Snohomish people established three villages on South Whidbey, including a large one near the head of Holmes Harbor. Food was generally abundant. Berries—salal, blackberry, soapberry, strawberry, serviceberry, cranberry, thimbleberry and huckleberry—were diet staples. So were nettles, which the tribe cultivated along with common camas, a type of edible bulb that they baked in a slow oven for hours. Reportedly, it tastes like garlic. Camas served as both a food source and major commodity for use in commerce with other tribes.

Each year in late May or June, when the berries had begun to ripen and camas bulbs were ready to dig, people left their permanent villages for seasonal sites. Extensive clam beds drew them to Baby Island, where they established summer homes, building mat houses and a sand dune fort for defense against potential raiders.

Baby Island is part of an ecosystem teeming with life. Clams, mussels, sea anemones, sponges, starfish, sea urchins, sand dollars and many other sea creatures are found in its tide flats. Harbor seals rest atop the island. Eagles, blue herons, cormorants and seagulls feed from the surrounding waters. Thousands of gulls and ducks make the island home during their respective migrating seasons. Orca pods travel through nearby Saratoga Passage.

In September, when the great fall runs of salmon began once again, people returned to their villages. Salmon—pinks, coho, chum, Chinook, sockeye—were thick in the waters of Holmes Harbor. It wasn't until after white people had settled that what had been thousands of salmon during a seasonal run began a dramatic decline in numbers as a result of growing pollution caused by runoff from logging operations. Farming practices that prevented access to spawning grounds and overfishing contributed as well.

ONLY WHAT WAS NEEDED

"Before we were human, we existed in a spiritual world" proclaims a banner on the wall of the Hibulb Cultural Center in Tulalip, Washington, where the story of the Tulalip tribes, a federation that now includes the Snohomish tribe, is told. The Snohomish people believe spirit lives exist in everything from the rocks and trees to salmon and other sea life, as well as in all the animals of the land.

These spiritual beliefs engender a natural respect for all things. Even as the Snohomish altered the lands around them to meet their needs, they managed their environment so as to sustain it. When fire and axes felled old-growth trees, for example, the Snohomish used every harvested part. Trunks and large limbs of the huge cedar trees became canoes, plank houses, carvings, totem poles, drums and storage boxes. They used bark for mats, baskets, clothing, towels, diapers and blankets. They used the wood from boughs for rope, medicines and bathing implements.

The Snohomish people actively worked to prevent food scarcity, something they understood well. Good stewardship of land and food resources was encouraged and rewarded. Pacific salmon, their most important food resource, is an example. Expert fisherman, they caught salmon with nets, harpoons and traps as the fish made the trip upstream to spawn—enough fish to last until the next year. They wanted to ensure a continuing and abundant future supply by making sure enough salmon survived and reached the spawning grounds.

CHANGE WITH THE WHITE SETTLERS

The 1855 Treaty of Point Elliott required the Snohomish and Snoqualmie tribes living on Whidbey Island to cede their ancestral lands, including Baby Island, and relocate to reservations. The Snohomish were promised continued access to their fishing grounds and a permanent reservation made up of two sections of land or 1,280 acres on Kwilt-seh-da (Snohomish Bay). These promises were never kept. But the Snohomish people continued to return to Baby Island until the late 1920s. They beached their canoes, spread their blankets on the sand and clamshell shelf and baked mussels and clams on hot rocks.

The Snohomish, like many hunter-gatherer societies, promoted common ownership of lands and other resources to manage them more effectively. The arriving white settlers brought a different cultural experience and sensibility. Theirs was a culture of private ownership and the right of individuals to exploit natural resources both to sustain themselves and their families and to foster economic development.

The settlers came with the dream of a new life. Federal land grant programs and the stories of settlers who preceded them encouraged them. They left behind farms that they had nourished in different climates and soils, not realizing that what they believed to be natural lands on Whidbey were actually the result of thousands of years of careful management practices by tribal people.

Eager to reestablish themselves, the settlers tried, as Walter Crockett, an early settler on Whidbey Island, expressed it, "to get the land subdued and the wilde nature out of it." They replaced or supplanted natural vegetation and wildlife with plants and animals considered more useful and economically productive. Some saw economic opportunity in the abundance of natural resources such as timber and furs and began systematically extracting them to sell in often faraway markets.

Baby Island, the quaint little island that sustained the Snohomish people for nearly a millennium, changed in a short space of time. In 1920, it became the site of a fishing resort with substantially more buildings and human activity on its small surface than ever before.

Darrell Scott first camped on Baby Island in 1910, when he and his father owned land on Whidbey Island's Dines Point. Injured in the torpedoing of a troopship off Scotland during World War I, Scott left his hospital bed against medical advice and came back to Whidbey Island. He decided he would spend whatever life he had left hunting, fishing and camping, and he

Baby Island becomes Darrell Scott's home, date unknown. *Courtesy of South Whidbey Island Historical Society.*

Darrell Scott's fish camp, date unknown. *Courtesy of South Whidbey Island Historical Society.*

took up residence on Baby Island. When Scott purchased the island in 1919, it was more than an acre in size.

Baby Island became Scott's year-round home. Moreover, it became his livelihood, the way in which he supported himself and his family. He built his house, along with a sprawling fishing lodge and tourist cabins, a configuration of structures that almost overwhelmed the small island. At times as many as twenty-five people were in residence on the island for short periods, having come to fish, clam, trap mink and vacation.

Scott worked hard. He housed and fed his visitors, sold bait and rented boats. He depended on wind-generated power and water that he hauled in kegs from a small stream just past Whidbey's Rocky Point, directly across from Baby Island, because the well he dug was brackish. Later, when Baby Island Heights was platted in that same area, he piped water across the few hundred feet to his island.

Over the years, Scott's rustic lodge attracted many visitors. Some arrived from Seattle on the *Atlantic*, a passenger steamer. The *Atlantic* would stop in the middle of the Saratoga Passage and drop passengers over the side into a waiting rowboat. They were then taken to the lodge or a rustic cabin where they could stay inexpensively. Ardent sportsmen often visited, and some, including well-known people such as Eddie Bauer, eventually built homes on Whidbey.

Scott's colorful tenure on Baby Island ended in a poker game at Langley's Dog House Tavern. He gambled and lost the island in 1937 to a man known only as "M. Hoard." Mr. Hoard tried and failed to fight the perpetual erosion that continued to diminish Baby Island by surrounding the island with a timbered bulkhead that has since disappeared. Mother Nature, aided by human activity, remained in control.

Shoreline development on Rocky Point and along Saratoga Beach, 2006. Concrete sea walls, prominent along the beach, shift the movement of sands that, in turn, affect Baby Island. *Courtesy of Washington State Department of Ecology.*

Baby Island, 2013. It has been reduced from approximately an acre in size, when the fish camp was operational, to eighty by two hundred feet today. *Courtesy of Michael Stadler Photography.*

On nearby Whidbey Island, people built homes along the water and added hard structures, including sea walls, on the beaches to protect their property. Sands shift constantly. Hard structures change that movement, allowing sand to build up in one place while increasing erosion in others. With continuing development along the Whidbey shoreline, Baby Island began to lose even more ground.

Buildings stood on the tiny island as late as the mid-1960s. Continuing erosion finally forced abandonment. Some cabins were moved to nearby Baby Island Heights on Whidbey Island, the site that had once been Scott's water source. The remaining buildings offered minimal shelter to campers and an occasional hardy resident until the early 1970s, when a heavy storm demolished all remnants of buildings and severely reduced the size of the island. Now Baby Island has reverted to the wild land it once was, albeit smaller and without the wild roses, snowballs and cherries.

Spirit Place Reclaimed

Ownership of Baby Island passed across several other people until 1993, when the Federation of Tulalip Tribes of Washington set out to reclaim a part of its heritage. It purchased Baby Island for $127,400.

Tribal lands today are managed within a complicated set of relationships among the U.S. Bureau of Indian Affairs, state and local governments and tribal governments. The Tulalip tribes negotiated for ten long years within this governmental network, trying to place their little island in trust. They planned to create a conservation easement and hoped to slow the island's erosion.

It has been an uphill battle. The complexities of land tenure and federal Indian law work against them. The land, although owned by the tribes, remains under local government control. That means the tribes cannot move forward without government permission. On the one hand, there are government policies designed to preserve and protect tribal land. On the other hand, there is pressure on policy makers to keep nonreservation land available for potential development. The tribes are caught in the middle.

Despite the challenges, it is fitting that this remarkable little island once again resides with the native peoples whose ancestors were nurtured by its abundant resources. The Snohomish people were gentle in their occupation; their presence did little to change the land. Perhaps they understand and respect, more than the white people who came after them, the powerful persistence of nature.

Visitors to Baby Island are allowed by the Tulalips who most likely recognize that their numbers will remain small. It is now a destination only for the lucky beachcomber or clam digger who happens upon a low minus tide and the occasional fisherman who arrives by boat at its diminishing shores.

3
The Maxwelton Watershed

Nutrient-rich from the spent bodies of salmon, the Maxwelton watershed for centuries sustained tall trees, wildlife and the native tribes who came to hunt and fish. White settlers eventually came. Farming practices and the gradual shift from a rural to a suburban environment affected the eco-environment of the watershed and, in particular, the salmon habitat. The dramatic drop in the salmon population is a stark indicator of the declining health of the watershed.

MAXWELTON CREEK BUBBLES ALONG on a twelve-mile journey through mixed conifer and wetland forests, peat bogs, agricultural lands and various culvert pipes that lead it under man-made structures such as roadways. The creek is the heart of the Maxwelton watershed, located on the southern end of Whidbey Island. It is the largest of seventy-two watersheds in Island County and covers 11.6 square miles (7,834 acres). The watershed extends north from Useless Bay about six miles into the interior of the island. State Highway 525, the main corridor across South Whidbey, divides it.

The persistent little creek, at times barely visible, begins its journey in the upper reaches of the watershed, where it is fed by several headwaters and underground springs. Along the way it branches into tributaries such as Quade Creek. It meanders through numerous peat deposits, partially decayed plant matter in wet ground—remnants of the last glacial era. Peat contains tannins that turn the water brown and inspire the nickname "Pepsi Cola Creek."

Aerial photo of Maxwelton Creek at the point where it forms a fresh water lake in the estuary before flowing into Useless Bay. *Courtesy of Washington State Department of Ecology.*

Maxwelton Creek finally arrives at Useless Bay on the west side of the island and forms an estuary, a combining of fresh and salt water. Creek water continues to flow into a near-shore marine environment along the adjacent shorelines and coastal bluffs that line the bay.

The creek is one of only two salmon-bearing creeks in Island County. Two species of salmon—coho (silver) and chum—are linked to the watershed, as well as one type of Pacific trout, the sea-run cutthroat. The estuary and near-shore marine environment create an important feeding and rearing stop for migrating salmon.

There is evidence that other young salmon—pink, chum and Chinook that hatch in the nearby Skagit and Snohomish Rivers—spend considerable time growing and feeding in the waters off Whidbey Island. The near-shore marine environment fed by Maxwelton Creek is an important nursery for them as well.

WATERSHEDS

We all live on a watershed—land that water flows across or under as it makes its way to a river, lake, stream or bay. Watersheds provide drinking water for humans and food and water for animals and plant life. They are living systems fed by all the rain that falls. Everything that happens on the land affects the quality of water as it drains into streams and flows downward.

The Maxwelton watershed hosts many habitats, including a riparian corridor, a unique plant habitat with diverse plant communities. A riparian corridor filters sediment from runoff before it enters rivers and streams, protects stream banks from erosion, maintains a storage area for periodic flooding and creates a habitat for fish and wildlife.

Rural hawks, coyotes, owls, raccoons, pheasants, ducks, songbirds and other wildlife make their home in the Maxwelton watershed. Beavers live in lodges that they build in the creek. Their presence is controversial; they help maintain a healthy salmon habitat, but the dams they construct pose a nuisance to farmers.

Healthy watersheds need undisturbed tree-lined stream banks and edges for filtering sediments and pollutants. The shade of foliage, tree roots and woody debris is important to keep water cool and provide habitat for fish and aquatic life. Human activity can seriously disturb the natural systems that keep water clean and fish healthy.

Salmon returning to spawn in the cool, shaded waters of a healthy creek. At one time, the sound of salmon returning to Maxwelton Creek to spawn was like the roar of a freight train. Now, they do not return in sustainable numbers. *Private collection.*

Human habitation has had a seriously negative impact on the health of the Maxwelton watershed. The declining numbers of salmon that return to Maxwelton Creek each year to spawn are stark evidence. In the past, tens of thousands of fish returned. Old-timers tell of being awakened by the sound of salmon, roaring like an advancing freight train, as they fought their way upstream. It was said that the creek swelled with salmon nearly to the point where a person could walk across the water on their backs. Today, the salmon population has dropped far below sustainable levels.

First Arrivals

Since ancient times, salmon returned to Maxwelton Creek to spawn, build nests (called redd) and lay eggs in the cool fresh water of the upper watershed. Some fifteen thousand years ago, the Vashon Glacier scoured out peaks and valleys on what would become Whidbey Island. As the mile-thick glacier slowly receded, much of the island remained under water for another four to five millennia until water levels in Puget Sound gradually lowered. Thin layers of gravel were laid down in streams. Salmon, believed to have survived glaciation in refuges on the North American and Asian continents, recolonized millions of miles of rivers and creeks in the Pacific Northwest.

After spawning, salmon die. Their bodies deposit nutrients that, in ancient times, helped reestablish vegetation, starting with western hemlock and red cedar, species that had survived the glaciation. Later, Sitka spruce grew up along the peat bogs. Red alder, ash and maple grew along flood plains, shorelines, rivers and the banks of the creek. Over time, an ecosystem began to support insects, birds, reptiles, amphibians, mammals and eventually people.

Salmon were a primary food source and an important part of the cultural heritage of the early glacier people who appeared ten to twelve thousand years ago. The Salish people who gradually replaced them around AD 1400 also celebrated and depended on salmon.

White settlers began to arrive on Whidbey Island in the mid-1800s, principally in the northern and central parts, where the land was most suited to cultivation. Salmon played a different role in the white culture. As a food source, salmon were commercialized. Overfishing combined with the pollution of waterways caused by logging operations began to affect the great runs of the past. Farmers introduced practices that changed salmon habitat. The numbers of salmon declined precipitously.

MAXWELTON VALLEY GROWTH

By 1860, the prairie lands in the center and north of Whidbey Island had mostly been claimed by white settlers. What remained were the marshland, tidelands and forests in the south. That's what settlers found when they got to the valley that would be named Maxwelton in the late 1800s and early 1900s.

Maxwelton—the town, valley and creek—owe their name to the Mackies, a farming family who settled in the area at the turn of the last century. Inspired by the old Scottish song "Annie Laurie," the family drew on lyrics that exclaim, "Maxwelton's braes are bonnie" to name their new home. The Mackies and other families who homesteaded in the beautiful valley created a solid and prosperous farming community.

By the time the Mackies got to the valley, timber companies had already been there. In the early days, the upper part of the Maxwelton watershed was marked by dense stands of old growth Douglas fir, hemlock and cedar. Timber men recognized the economic value of these old-growth forests, and the timber industry in the valley grew quickly. Logging at the time was primitive and wasteful. Lots of timber was left on the forest floor at the end of a logging operation, hampering tree regeneration. Within twenty years, much of the valley had been logged.

The land use pattern that developed supported farming families but eroded salmon habitat. Timber companies purchased land, logged it and

Horse-drawn rail cart carries logs from the forest to a mill in the Maxwelton watershed, circa 1887–89. *Courtesy of South Whidbey Island Historical Society.*

then sold it to those who wanted to farm. Farmers learned to grow crops on land filled with the stumps and slash of logged trees. The acidic, infertile soils were more suited to tree growth than food crops and highly vulnerable to degradation. The most fertile soils were the tidelands, important to the life cycle of the salmon. But the tidelands were regularly washed by seawater. To manage saltwater intrusion, farmers built dikes and tide gates, and they planted in the rich soils of the estuary.

Social patterns also changed. In the early days, hardworking farmers in the lower Maxwelton Valley produced more bushels of oats per acre than anywhere else in the nation. But by the mid-1950s, the number of farms had dwindled. People began to come from urban environments for a more rural way of life. Attracted by the beauty of the area, they purchased old homesteads or newly developed lots and built modern homes surrounded by lawns and gardens. The ferry provided easy access, and some enjoyed their island homes while maintaining residences on the nearby mainland.

Today, farm fields, residential dwellings and second- and third-growth timber fill the Maxwelton watershed. More than 150 landowners now control the future of the creek. Housing fills the estuary. About fifteen families still live on land homesteaded by their pioneering ancestors. Their farming practices are controversial, but their presence over time has helped to prevent more dense development.

SALMON DECLINE

Human presence on the watershed has damaged the fragile environment. People have removed and destroyed natural vegetation in the riparian corridor along the creek, tilled and planted right to the edge of the creek, and kept the creek flowing for crops, residential gardens and thirsty cattle. Native trees and shrubs have been removed to make pastureland or groomed lawn, which has increased erosion. Over-fertilization of lawns, excess manure application to fields, failed septic systems, illicit pipe connections—all these threaten aquatic life, including salmon, and contaminate water.

Land use changes such as diking and the construction of tide gates quickly kills off saltwater-dependent marsh fish such as salmon, herring, and perch as well as invertebrates such as clams and mussels. This die-off, in turn, decreases the food supply for marsh birds. The absence of salt water also causes vegetation to shift dramatically from salt grasses to freshwater plants.

Removing drainage tile from an abandoned farm field. The underground pipes once kept the field dry by moving the water away from the wetland soils, altering the habitat. *Courtesy of Whidbey Watershed Stewards.*

Salmon that began life in Maxwelton Creek return to spawn. They stop at the mouth of the creek to feed and readjust to fresh water in preparation for the demanding trip upstream to their spawning grounds. The tide gates stop nearly all of them. People tell stories of salmon throwing themselves against the tide gates in a futile effort to gain access to their spawning areas.

The few salmon that are able to make it past the tide gates face other dangers. Salmon eggs need to incubate for one to three months in gravel spawning beds, washed over by cold, clean, oxygen-rich water. Deforestation, cultivation too near the streambed, and increased erosion cause silt and sand to cover the thin layer of gravel, making it difficult for the salmon to spawn.

Baby salmon, called alevins, absorb nutrients from their attached yolk sac and grow into fry. The coho fry hatch and remain in the upper watershed for up to two years and then migrate to salt water. Chum fry make their way down to the lower watershed almost immediately. Sea-run cutthroats travel back and forth between fresh and salt waters, spawning in the fresh water and feeding in the salt water.

Eventually fry leave the protection of the rocks to live and grow in the current of the water until they are able to make the transition from fresh water to salt water, a process called smolting. If trees and other vegetation no longer shade the creek water, it may become warm and deoxygenated, making it impossible for smolt to survive as they grow and migrate to the sea for the first time.

The estuary is vital to the smolt. There they transition from fresh water to sea water, begin to feed on minute zooplankton and, gradually, on larger creatures such as crustaceans and shrimp. At one time, the saltwater estuary created by Maxwelton Creek swelled up to two hundred acres in size during high tides. So many salmon returned each year that commercial and native salmon wheels were set up throughout the tidelands, and a fish processing facility was built at the mouth of the creek. Today, the estuary is roughly two or three acres in size, and most of the time it is filled with fresh water.

One's Solution, Another's Problem

In 1990, the State of Washington passed the Growth Management Act. It requires local governments to identify and protect critical areas and natural resource lands, designate urban growth areas, prepare comprehensive plans and implement them through capital investments and development regulations.

Island County developed regulations specific to long-term watershed recovery. But many of the regulations run counter to the way farmers have always done things. For many years, farmers had employed practices that kept Maxwelton Creek from drying up. New regulations prevented them from doing what they had always done. They are no longer allowed to remove accumulating plants and debris that, the farmers argue, make it hard to keep an adequate water supply year-round. When plants are allowed to rot in the water it becomes deoxygenated, they say, making it unhealthy for cattle to drink. Environmentalists argue that the dried-up creek and the natural debris are part of a long-term process of restoring the watershed.

Regulations also prevent the destruction of beaver dams. Environmentalists contend that beaver dams create ponds and store water that is then released over the drier summer months to the benefit of salmon. Farmers point out that beaver dams flood pastures and compromise agricultural fields.

In 1988, two years before passage of the Growth Management Act, salmon were on the minds of children attending South Whidbey's Intermediate

Children stand in Maxwelton Creek near the outdoor classroom and learn about the salmon life cycle. *Courtesy of Whidbey Watershed Stewards.*

School. Led by fifth grade teacher Rene Neff, they went to the hatchery for salmon eggs to plant in Maxwelton Creek. Rene's goal was to teach children about the life cycle of salmon and impress on them the important role of habitat. The idea for the project began with Bruce Bocte, whose daughter was one of the Rene's students. Within two years, students, teachers, and local residents had set up egg boxes and begun raising salmon in the creek. They monitored water quality and watched for signs of salmon returning to spawn. But their work was not done.

Through Rene's efforts, and with help from others, the Salmon Adventure was born. Local philanthropist Nancy Nordhoff contributed, as did Island County government through a newly developed Conservation Futures Fund. The Trust for Public Lands, a national land preservation organization, assisted with early financing. The project purchased just over six acres of land near Maxwelton Creek.

The local Rotary raised money by selling tiles with a fish motif and built an outdoor classroom where a steady stream of kindergarten through fifth graders learn about the types of salmon, their life cycle and the habitats that are their home when they return to fresh water. Children participated in school-based fundraisers. Community members pitched in to build a trail system. Since 1997, the Salmon Adventure property and classroom have been owned by the South Whidbey School District, which purchased them with an agreement that the district maintain the property and that Salmon Adventure continue to provide education for district students. The classroom also serves as a community gathering place for teacher retreats and adult classes.

Adults involved with the Salmon Adventure had friends who belonged to another local environmental group called Beach Watchers. These friends joined together and created a third group specifically to work on restoring salmon habitat in the Maxwelton watershed. They called themselves the Chums of the Salmon Adventure. This new group approached members of the local community to ask for changes in farming and residential practices that would support restoration efforts. Opposition mounted as concerns grew about the legacy rights of farmers and individual rights of property owners.

Change comes hard. Although many people supported the restoration work, some descendants of the original farm families, in particular, were reluctant to change practices that had existed for decades. Other property owners were concerned about losing their right to manage their property as they see fit. There were still bad feelings among some about the Growth Management Act.

The Chums invited experts in to evaluate the situation. Given the dramatic changes that had taken place in the estuary and lower watershed, and the controversy over proposed solutions, the expert team suggested a shift in focus away from the more populated lower watershed to the uplands, where the watershed begins. They also proposed an emphasis on the riparian buffers along the creek.

Today, the Chums have reorganized as the Whidbey Watershed Stewards (WWS). They still work on habitat restoration along the creek in the lower valley, but their efforts are now concentrated in the upper watershed. They also expanded their mission to include all of South Whidbey watershed and near shore marine environments.

More Work and Challenges

In 1999, the Whidbey Camano Land Trust, with the help of Nancy Nordhoff, brought a twenty-four-acre portion of wetlands—the Maxwelton Preserve—under its protection. The preserve includes a portion of Maxwelton Creek. Volunteers have begun an intensive stream restoration project that includes removing nonnative vegetation and restoring more than five hundred native plant species with the goal of re-creating a stream canopy. They also monitor the active beaver dams in this section.

In 2003, the WWS began conducting stream surveys of Maxwelton Creek to identify types and locations of fish in the stream system and recommend replacement of several road culverts that blocked fish passage. Their findings helped persuade private homeowners to replace culverts that blocked salmon movement. They also shared their findings with the Island County Public Works Department, which uses the information to assign priorities in its own culvert replacement schedule.

In 2007, the Whidbey Camano Land Trust partnered with the Washington State Department of Natural Resources to transfer 205 acres of wildlife and riparian habitat in the upper Maxwelton watershed to the South Whidbey Parks and Recreation District. It is now known as Trustland Trails. This area of mature forest includes the headwaters of Maxwelton Creek. Protection of the headwaters will help to preserve the overall condition of the watershed.

Challenges remain. In 2006, WWS volunteers began to conduct annual surveys in selected parts of Maxwelton Creek to count the number of salmon who return to spawn. Over the past seven years, the surveys show a continuing decline of smolt. Few salmon are returning.

Recently, the Washington State Department of Health closed public beaches and tidelands near the outfall of Maxwelton Creek to shellfish harvest. The problem is high bacteria levels, due in large measure to animal waste and failing septic systems. An area south of the outfall is listed as "impaired water." Island County Public Health began sampling in the Maxwelton watershed in May 2011 and will continue sampling through 2014. The goal is to improve surface water quality within the watershed and reopen recreational shellfish harvesting near the outfall of the creek.

COMPETING INTERESTS AND PERSPECTIVES

Everyone who lives in the Maxwelton Valley cares about the watershed. It's just that different groups have different visions of what needs protecting and how it should be done. The problem is one of competing economic interests and different perspectives about historic farming practices. Their challenge is to learn to compromise and manage the land collaboratively. Many communities in the Pacific Northwest face the same problems.

Nature, however, doesn't negotiate. A painful example is nearby Glendale Creek, located in the Glendale watershed. Salmon had been blocked from the upper reaches of the creek since the installation of a forty-eight-inch culvert beneath Glendale Road in the 1960s. A winter storm in January 1997 brought severe flooding that caused Glendale Road to collapse in several places, washed out culverts, and damaged homes in the Glendale community. But the creek became fish-friendly once again as wild and hatchery-raised salmon began to return. Larger culverts and other fish-friendly repairs were made to the flood-prone road. Salmon habitat has been protected in subsequent flood repairs as well.

Scientists from the University of Washington were invited to study the challenges that make it difficult to restore salmon habitat in Maxwelton Creek. Their conclusion was that, at this point in time, population growth and farming practices that compromise habitat make the problems nearly intractable. They noted that the region is at risk for tsunami conditions and that Mother Nature would, indeed, eventually deliver the ultimate solution. But in the meantime, many people still work on less volatile day-to-day resolutions.

4
Bayview

*A*n area emanating from a small crossroads called Bayview Corner on South Whidbey
Island is—and has been from its earliest days—a significant "place" for many: a
thriving locale of repurposing and a locus of community energy and assembly.

BAYVIEW WAS FROM EARLY post-settlement times a heavily forested commercial
center with a wharf for people and cargo. Looking south from the wharf, you
could see a spectacular view of Useless Bay and a six-hundred-acre estuary.
Bayview was named for this beautiful water vista. But because of human activity
and economic choices about altering the land through logging and diking, it is
no longer possible to see either the bay or what remains of the lagoon.

Until the early 1900s, you could use shallow-draft boats or canoes to travel
a short distance from Useless Bay, through the tidal estuary of Deer Lagoon to
within a half mile of the deep forest surrounding Lone Lake. Both native people
and early white settlers regularly made this journey to what is now Bayview. At
high tide, the water was about three feet deep.

Bayview is no longer a forest or a port. Although it has remained a commercial
center, its topography is now landlocked pastures. Its water view is a distant
memory. Yet it remains a source of rebuilding, incubation of ideas, conscious
sustainability, symbiosis and celebration. The community has repeatedly rallied
with a spirit of activism to maintain its essence as a gathering place where all
are welcome and each person's unique contribution is honored.

New Again

The first white settlers in Bayview built structures that brought people together, such as the first community hall in the 1880s. The oldest structure still standing in the area is a schoolhouse built around 1909, to replace older schools that had been in the vicinity from the early days of white settlement. This building has been many things over time: a school, an American Legion hall, a branch of Skagit Valley Community College, an alternative high school and now the Whidbey Island Community Education Center, which provides continuing education classes and workshops to community members of all ages.

In 1905, settlers donated land for the Bayview Cemetery where islanders would be interred in a community setting rather than individually on family farms as had been the custom.

The Bayview Cash Store, originally built in 1908 north of the small wharf at the outfall of Lone Lake, has had almost continuous service as a general store and community meeting place. (It was out of use for eight years following a 1916 fire before being rebuilt at its current location in 1924.) The Bayview Community Hall has hosted parties, artistic events, dances and other community gatherings since it opened in 1927. The Sears House, a farmworker's home built in 1914 from a kit sold through the Sears catalogue,

Bayview Cash Store in its early days, probably circa late 1920s. *Courtesy of Goosefoot.*

was moved to Bayview in 2001 from the Greenbank Farm. Now beautifully restored, it serves as a chiropractor's office and a gathering place for health and wellness education.

Every Saturday, spring through fall, the Bayview Farmers' Market draws locals and tourists for fresh, local produce, crafts, music and flowers. Bayview Farm and Garden, a 1993 addition to the area, is an important resource for the many gardeners and vegetable growers of the community and a vibrant, beautiful place throughout the year. An important presence at Bayview is the Good Cheer Food Bank and Community Garden, which draws people of diverse backgrounds and means together as neighbors to ensure everyone has access to healthy food.

Another Bayview neighbor is the Whidbey Telecom Company. It began in 1908, started by a group of South Whidbey business people and farmers. It was purchased by the Henny family in 1953 and is still owned by them. Today, it is known for being one of the few remaining privately owned telephone companies in the country and the first local company in the United States to bury 100 percent of its phone lines. At its campus built in 1960 near the original Bayview Wharf, the company flies a large, well-lit American flag around the clock.

Locals appreciate Whidbey Telecom for its involvement in the community and local philanthropy, but they are bemused that only calls from South Whidbey up to Greenbank at the middle of the island are billed as local calls. Beyond that, it's long distance rates into the territory of another phone company. There is a quirky exception: Whidbey Telecom also serves the U.S. community of Point Roberts, a little peninsula that extends southward from mainland Canada into Puget Sound, designated American in compliance with the international border at the forty-fifth parallel. It's 135 miles away from Bayview, but South Whidbey people can make a local call there too!

Not all of Bayview is of compelling historic or aesthetic interest. The area contains a modern mix of businesses, including a small family-run garage, a large compound of self-storage buildings, a grocery store and a hardware store. A few miles away, the Useless Bay Colony encompasses homes built on shoreline and bluff, with the Useless Bay Golf and Country Club providing another kind of social hub for many.

Bayview's growth and development over the past 150 years illustrate many aspects of peoples' impact on the land. Human intervention—particularly economic drivers such as logging and diking to "reclaim" farmland from the sea—changed the face of the area quickly and irrevocably. But in spite of this, it has remained a place in peoples' hearts and minds. It demonstrates how environmental protection and historic preservation have become more predominant community values on Whidbey Island.

Despite the fact its name is no longer a geographic eponym, Bayview remains a source of renewal and determination, rebuilding and repurposing, incubating ideas, conscious sustainability, symbiosis and celebration. It continues to inspire a call to service and activism in people of the community who work together to maintain its essence as a gathering place where all are welcome and all can make unique contributions.

About the Water

To understand Bayview, one needs to know about a bay, a lagoon, an estuary and a lake.

Let's start with the bay. Useless Bay is a large semicircle of water on the island's south end. It is shallow, surrounded by sandy beaches and tends to be warmer than nearby waters because it retains the warmth of the sun.

Useless Bay was named in 1841 by a U.S. Navy lieutenant and explorer, Charles Wilkes, who noted that the bay, however warm it might be, lacked shelter for vessels in a storm. He also observed that low tide removed enough water to expose the bottom in places so ships would be temporarily marooned. These observations are immortalized on many local baseball hats and polo shirts; the logo of the Useless Bay Golf and Country Club is a listing schooner, leaning precipitously to one side as the treacherous tide isolates it. Place names as well as histories are written by the winners. No pre-settlement Native American inhabitant would have considered this large, shellfish-rich, and usually calm bay as "useless."

On the land side, the bay borders a lagoon that was once surrounded by old-growth forest interspersed with wild grasses that supported large populations of deer. This led to another eponymous place name: Deer Lagoon. The lagoon in turn transitioned into a tidal estuary. This thriving ecosystem was a prolific food source full of shellfish and fish and water fowl for Indian people and later for white hunters and fishers.

Less than a mile north of Bayview is the little (ninety-two-acre) Lone Lake, whose outfall once nourished the lagoon and estuary. There are several other lakes nearby, so its name may have been bestowed as a reflection of some lonely pioneer's state of mind rather than any geographic singularity.

Surrounded by old-growth forest at the time of settlement, Lone Lake offered another economic incentive to white pioneers to settle this area as they came to its shores to log and process the bounty of the forest.

CHANGING PRIORITIES

Then came the dikes.

Decisions to dike in Deer Lagoon illustrate how settlers' priorities began to focus on arable land. Water transportation, the initial economic driver, became less important to the settlers as better roads were constructed and they were able to move themselves and their goods on land.

People built the dikes to keep the high tide out of some of the land around Deer Lagoon and to control sand drift from Useless Bay. The first pile dikes reclaimed some land but did not affect waterborne transportation from Useless Bay to Bayview.

It was the construction of two levee dikes in 1915 that cut Bayview off from the water. A one-third-mile-long levee cut off the east end of Deer Lagoon and created 480 acres of farmland, draining marshes and exposing land that didn't require the removal of stumps left from logging. A second dike on the west end of Deer Lagoon drained marshes and created another 386 acres of farmland. Water flowed through tunnels in the dikes and a system of tide gates allowed for slough water to flow out and prevented salt water from coming in at high tide.

Gradually, once worthless sandy beaches became prime real estate. The value of somewhat marshy farmland declined as beachfront became more and more valued by developers. Beach lots that were once a hard sell at fifty dollars a lot were now worth hundreds of thousands of dollars.

The original diking and outflow systems remained essentially intact until 2009, when concerns began to be raised that in the event of a major storm, the system would be unable to protect some of the reclaimed land where people had built houses. Amid disagreements over assessments from the Diking District and still unresolved lawsuits, a new pump was installed to better control the effects of weather and tides on low-lying areas.

A Little Culture Skirmish

Deer Lagoon was recently at the center of a controversy that points out how one group can replace another in political power. People had always hunted ducks on Deer Lagoon, following the earlier practice of Native American hunters and white settlers. In the 1980s, the property owner (the developer of Useless Bay Colony) imposed a hunting ban in the area, citing the safety of nearby residences abutting the lagoon on three sides. That ban was defiantly and dangerously ignored. Prohibitive signs were torn down, and enforcers reported that some hunters pointed guns at them when they were confronted.

Island County purchased the land in 2004 and, bowing to custom, opened the area to hunting once again.

But in 2009, population density around the lagoon and shifting political clout between old-timers and newer residents with more suburban expectations reached critical mass. The county ended traditional hunting there after extensive, emotional and divisive debate. "We're not the island we were," said a county commissioner at the time. "We're talking about mixing a neighborhood with firearms." So Useless Bay and its lagoon became "useless" to another group of people, newly marginalized in an ever-evolving community.

From Timber to Farms

Human intention, industry and economic incentive dramatically change any natural environment. Logging—driven by all three of these factors—was the first major industry on South Whidbey, and it quickly changed the land around Bayview.

Native people had long engaged in selective burning of forests to encourage the growth of desirable food. This practice was small scale, and forests quickly recovered. But from 1850 to 1920, the scale of logging increased to meet high demand for timber. This forever altered the landscape. Logs were shipped to rapidly growing urban centers for construction and for use in other industries, such as support poles to be used in mines. Woodcutters produced building shingles and provisioned the inefficient wood-gobbling steamers that serviced the island. The trees that fell were huge: some as high as three hundred feet and as thick as fifteen feet in diameter.

By 1870, thirteen logging camps operated on South Whidbey, including one in Bayview. Initially, logs were skidded to the water using oxen, secured into booms and towed off-island to larger mills. As the logging moved farther away from the water, transportation of logs to off-island processing became more difficult. Soon a mill was built on the east side of Useless Bay and another constructed by Lone Lake.

The volume of the logging continued to grow as more efficient techniques and machinery were developed. Logging of old-growth timber continued into the 1920s, gradually opening up land for farming and pastureland.

DEVELOPMENT ONE WAY OR ANOTHER

The placement and construction of the Whidbey Island's main road (State Highway 525) in the late 1950s cut off Bayview Corner, bypassing the Bayview Cash Store and its environs. Still, islanders continued to gather in their historic community hub. The Cash Store, the nursery and various small businesses and galleries thrived, and the farmers' market flourished. Bayview School and Bayview Hall continued to draw people of all ages.

But people were gradually developing a sense of unease about the vigorous development transforming Whidbey Island landscapes. There was growing fear about the loss of a cherished way of life as the island rapidly changed. One need travel no further than fifteen minutes by ferry to see the effects of sprawl and the steady loss of places where people felt welcome and known. "We don't want to become like Lynnwood" was often heard, as islanders drove off the ferry on the other side into the wilderness of strip malls, fast food franchises, pedestrian-unfriendly thoroughfares and a dearth of natural beauty and open space.

In the mid-1990s, a small but passionate group of islanders successfully fought against the fast-food giant McDonald's, which was expressing interest in franchising in the Bayview area. This was a symbol to many islanders of what they feared most in their community: the loss of a rural quality of life. It would mean anonymous fast food rather than their own beloved mom-and-pop eateries and a multinational corporate toehold in a place that valued home-grown entrepreneurship.

Students of South Whidbey High School, led by the Ecology Club, actively protested. They wrote letters to the editor and painted their vehicle windows with the international "banned" sign of a circle with a slash across golden arches. Others joined the protest. McDonald's ultimately withdrew, either because of the community's distaste for what the fast-food culture represented or the intractable septic and water issues that became more trouble than the market was worth.

A similar protest had earlier erupted in 1994 when Dairy Queen wanted to go into business on the island. But that protest couldn't stop this fast-food franchise from being built near the ferry in Clinton.

A long and controversial protest arose as the county considered the permitting of a gas station on what some activists believed to be a wetland a few miles north of Bayview in Freeland. After a lengthy delay, property owners were able to convince county officials that the property was not a wetland, opening the way for construction to begin. Protesters picketed during the building phase, angry about development being prioritized over environment. The gas station duly opened in June 2008. Today, many islanders refuse to buy gas there to show their continued opposition, while some buy gas expressly to show support for private property rights. Thus, the controversy continues, just more quietly.

But even before these incidents, much larger projects had been at play that drew islanders' attention.

USELESS BAY COLONY

The Sievers family had been coming to Whidbey Island every summer since the 1930s to a little fishing cabin made from a gas station they had barged over from the mainland. Family patriarch Howard Sievers, a surveyor and later a sand and gravel magnate, started his island real estate development career by trading a surveying fee for four hundred feet of bayfront property. Patiently, he accumulated other properties and eventually incorporated H&H Properties in 1959.

In the early '60s, the company submitted a plan to the county to develop around 1,000 acres (five hundred lots) in the Useless Bay area along shorelines and the bluff overlooking the bay. The development included a 150-acre, eighteen-hole golf course. Excavating reclaimed marginal farmland provided fill for the back nine fairways and created small lakes for the course.

Initially, the development was to be a lagoon community along the shoreline with a marina and boat slips for the homes, but plans had to be modified in the '70s, when a land use case from Lake Chelan set a statewide precedent preventing the requisite bulk-heading and land fill.

H&H had expected that many homes in the Useless Bay Colony would be small second homes, more like the Sieverses' original fishing cabin. But the real estate boom of the 1980s and '90s created a market for larger homes designed for year-round occupancy. On the Useless Bay beaches, these unexpectedly spacious homes were now crowded together on lots designed to accommodate cabins. There are also many large second or even third homes in the colony.

Even with the unanticipated effects of the real estate market on Useless Bay Colony, the Sieverses saw themselves guiding the growth carefully and thoughtfully. They buried power lines and ensured infrastructure was more than adequate. So they were surprised about the push-back they got from some community members about the development, even though they felt they were members of the community themselves and not "outsiders." Patty Sievers recalls how opinions hardened then on what development, if any, would be welcome or even possible on South Whidbey Island.

Retouching Grass Roots

In the late '90s, Bayview became the site of community renewal in a visionary effort that would be known as Goosefoot. Goosefoot would come to make significant contributions to the look, livability and economic success of South Whidbey Island.

By 1998, the islanders' worries about impending changes and potential loss of something precious was palpable. Troubling rumors became threatening reality as the landowner of the acreage at the heart of Bayview Corner announced his property was up for sale.

What would happen to the Cash Store, the farmers' market and the nursery? There was talk of the Cash Store being razed. People were increasingly watchful, wary and energized. As Debbie Torget, then the manager of the farmers' market, said, "People didn't want to lose their place. This area became the place to make a stand."

The stand began with a casual conversation in the parking lot of the Cash Store. Local philanthropist Nancy Nordhoff chatted with Linda Moore, a real estate attorney who had recently moved to the island. They discussed the impending property sale and the various development scenarios that were gaining momentum and asked each other, "What are we going to do?" They realized that saving the Cash Store was the first piece of the puzzle. They instinctively understood Winston Churchill's warning: "We shape our buildings, and afterwards, our buildings shape us." The Cash Store had played an important role in the shaping of the South Whidbey community. Now it was time to ensure its longevity.

The women understood that they would have to buy the land that was up for sale. Because of the inadequacy of the existing septic and surface water management systems, additional nearby land would be needed to upgrade the systems. They would need to take on complicated and expensive mitigation of derelict underground gasoline storage tanks on the site.

Nordhoff sums up the partnership by saying, "We made a commitment" to prevent the destruction of Bayview Cash Store and grounds "and to think about what needed to happen instead. Linda had the expertise, imagination and energy. I had the money."

A compelling combination of geography, history and feeling of place spurred them on. They began using the term "gathering place" in their conversations—a fairly common term now but unusual then. They knew they wanted to nourish the community tradition of coming together both physically and psychologically at Bayview.

The two women formed the Bayview Cash Store LLC. Within a week, it was changed to Bayview Corner LLC. On March 13, 1999, it became Goosefoot. Nordhoff had earlier formed Orach, a corporation named after a hearty plant that is a member of the Goosefoot family, to buy land for a public park in Langley. The Orach board became the initial board of Goosefoot.

Goosefoot's mission was and is to preserve rural traditions, to enhance local commerce, to build a sense of place and community and to create a sustainable future. These are lofty ideas. As always, the devil is in the details.

Not all islanders agreed with Goosefoot's strategies and decisions. Some backlash was personal and ugly. One man bitterly declaimed the planned remodel of the Cash Store, wanting no change at all and claiming Goosefoot plans amounted to a "sleazy strip mall." The Smilin' Dog, a popular coffee shop at the Cash Store, vacated in 2006 over the terms of their lease, a development that still generates some bad feelings in the community. Change of any kind elicits strong reactions.

But Goosefoot continued by being "agile and doing educated risk taking," according to Marian Myszkowski, Goosefoot's director of program and fund development.

Remodeled Cash Store used many recycled materials, 2012. *Courtesy of Goosefoot.*

"We began to understand we could not be everything for everybody but could offer something for everybody," remembers Torget, who ultimately became Goosefoot's executive director. "The central metaphor is 'barn raising,' not 'the old west.' It is about the rural values of coming together as a community, building something, helping each other out. It's not independent action, cut off from neighbors. [It's] see a neighbor's need, take an action."

ACTION AND ACHIEVEMENT

In 1999, Goosefoot purchased the Cash Store and eight adjoining acres. Next, it restored and remodeled the Cash Store. Goosefoot formed its own construction company and became a significant employer of local craftspeople and artisans who worked with recycled materials and environmentally friendly infrastructure.

That year, the organization provided low-cost financing to Bayview Farm and Garden to enable the nursery to purchase land for expansion. In 2001, Goosefoot moved the Sears kit house from Greenbank Farm. In 2002, it completed the house's restoration using recycled materials and sustainable building practices. By 2002, Goosefoot had purchased twenty-two acres of land at the Bayview Corner. In 2004, it completed the Cash Store remodel and restoration, and the structure now houses a variety of locally owned businesses and nonprofit organizations.

In 2005, Goosefoot purchased nine acres at Bayview Center, a small commercial development containing a Red Apple grocery store across the highway from Bayview Corner. In 2008, Red Apple decided not to renew its lease for the store, and Goosefoot began a search for a new grocery tenant. Unable to find one, it entered into an agreement with the Whidbey-based Myers Group to manage it. The new grocery store, the Goose, opened in September 2009. It offers affordable prices on basics and makes a commitment to carrying locally grown and produced products. The market also makes substantial food and product donations to local nonprofit agencies. In a short time, it has become a popular community asset.

Goosefoot uses and demonstrates "green" development practices for others, including shared infrastructure such as parking and common surface water management strategies developed with neighbors. It modeled the creative use of recycled materials and zero waste on the Cash Store remodel, even purchasing the defunct Langley Water Tower to use its beautiful old redwood in the Sears House and the Cash Store.

Not all its dreams have come true. Goosefoot was committed from its earliest days to affordable housing for working people. Bayview seemed the perfect place for it, with its nearby services and bus routes. The organization was awarded nearly $2 million in low-income tax credits and had solved the daunting problems of soil constraints and septic capacity. Ultimately, the effort was halted in the face of community concerns and some environmental activists' antipathy toward densely populated housing development, no matter how carefully and sensitively designed.

For fourteen years, Goosefoot has focused its efforts on building community by encouraging cooperation among businesses as neighbors, assisting and nurturing new locally owned businesses and creating spaces and events where people feel known and welcome. It is a modern reconstruction of the community that has long existed at Bayview, a collective repurposing of a history-laden place. It affirms the human connections that have made it special over so many years.

"What begins as undifferentiated space becomes place as we get to know it better and endow it with value," says philosopher and geographer Yi-Fu Tuan. When we begin to make changes and pathways through our landscape, it becomes even more deeply our own.

Street dance at Bayview Corner, one of many community events at this thriving gathering place. *Courtesy of Goosefoot.*

Bayview's particular vibrancy comes from dynamic forces at work there: history, creativity, inclusiveness, longstanding relationships, financial wherewithal and a certain shared way of being in the world—a rare and powerful synthesis.

5

Greenbank Farm

*A*t the 151-acre Greenbank Farm, basic human needs for food, recreation and community are reimagined in a beloved and diverse natural environment. The farm's operations are coordinated by private-public governance in cooperation with its neighbors: nearby residents, Island County, the U.S. Navy and the Nature Conservancy.

As WHIDBEY ISLAND TWISTS and turns, it compresses at its middle to its narrowest point near Greenbank Farm. The farm's location, easily accessible from either end of the island and by canoe from nearby shores, made it a historic meeting place for indigenous people. Its breathtaking views of sea, mountain and nearby islands make it a destination for hikers and artists. Turning east, you can see Holmes Harbor, Camano Island, Baby Island and the Saratoga Passage, with the Cascades Range sparkling in the distance. To the west are the Straits of Juan de Fuca, the city of Port Townsend and another gleaming mountain range, the Olympics.

The island's main highway skirts along the gentle slope of the farm, giving travelers a calming vision of open fields, pond, gardens, grazing animals and historic farm buildings. A row of solar panels, a new kind of crop, gleams out in the pasture. Recognizing the beauty to be seen here and elsewhere along the highway, the U.S. secretary of transportation designated it as one of American's Scenic Byways, named Whidbey Scenic Isle Way.

Often signs and bright banners catch the eye, alerting passersby to festivals, farmers' markets, art gallery activities and other community events. If it is summer and car windows are open, you can sometimes hear music or the

Greenbank Farm from the air. Greenbank developed on the shores of Holmes Harbor but now clusters around Greenbank Store along Highway 525. *Courtesy of Washington State Department of Ecology.*

sounds of excited announcers giving a play by play at a dog agility course or calling children to a pie-eating contest.

Greenbank Farm may rest physically on a narrow spot, but it shelters bold vision. It is the culmination of the creative efforts of all those who lived there, developed the farm, shepherded it through changes across the years and are now working to understand, preserve and deepen its heritage. It is a place of meaning and community identity to the many islanders who mobilized to save it from destruction in the 1990s.

THE LAND LIVES

As is the case with many iconic Whidbey locations, this place has been many things to many people over time. The lands now containing Greenbank Farm were part of the traditional homeland of the Skagit tribe on Whidbey Island. As this location was close to the border of lands claimed by the Snohomish tribe just to the south, it is said to have been a place of peaceful meeting, potlatches and trade between the tribes. It was also revered as a place of burial for tribal ancestors.

The Skagit and Snohomish were each part of the larger Coast Salish group, at one point classified by anthropologists as "Canoe" or "Saltwater" Indians. The Coast Salish inhabited a large geographic area, comprising some First Nations groups in British Columbia and many tribes of Native Americans living in Washington and Oregon. The Skagit and the Snohomish were closely related physically and linguistically but differed in dialects, kinship patterns and traditions.

Both tribes had permanent villages with wood longhouses and seasonal camps for harvesting plants and animals as they became available in their annual cycle. In addition to being hunters, gatherers and fishers, they were farmers in the sense that they conducted periodic burning of prairies to increase the growth of preferred plants, notably bracken and camas. As historian Richard White writes:

> *In the eyes of the Salish, not only humans, plants and animals occupied this land, but also a vast array of spirits associated with specific animals or natural phenomena. This added dimension gave the land an ambience and meaning it largely lacked for whites... They populated this land with spirits and powers, but they did not restrict their manipulation to magic. Through observation and tradition, Indians altered natural communities to fit their needs without, in the process, destroying the ability of those communities to sustain the cultures that had created them.*

THE COMMUNITY

Greenbank got its name from its founder, Calvin Philips, originally from Greenbank, Delaware. Philips named this new community in homage to his birthplace (spelled Green Bank in his 1958 *Seattle Times* obituary).

Philips moved from Philadelphia to Washington State in late 1891 and established a real estate and property-management business in Tacoma. Later, he became involved in speculation related to lands released for sale by railroads. The federal government granted much land along each side of proposed routes west to the railroad companies to encourage westward expansion and settlement. At one point, Whidbey Island had been seriously considered for the northwest terminus of the transcontinental railroad.

Tacoma was ultimately chosen, but only after considerable speculative land acquisition on Whidbey before the final decision was made.

Philips was in business with partners on the East Coast to buy and sell extraneous railroad property at what was expected to be great profit. He planned to sell ten thousand acres the partnership had acquired on Whidbey Island, and for a while, things seemed to go well—selling five thousand in only a month. But the economic depression of the 1890s adversely affected plans for continued easy profit.

In the early 1900s, Philips bought 1,500 acres on Whidbey Island for himself, named the area Greenbank and set about developing it as a compelling demonstration of the value of the property to potential buyers.

The area was still heavily forested but contained cleared farmland and beachfront along Holmes Harbor that could support water transport. And it was already a community: a school had been operating in the area since 1901. The first white settlers were said to have arrived in 1889.

Philips built a wharf on the south end of the Greenbank beach for passengers and cargo. He constructed a two-story hotel for tourists and sited a store and post office within it before building another structure nearby for this purpose. By 1909, the area was served by steamer three times a week. It was a busy place, and by 1913, daily steamer service was routine.

The community continued to grow. As roads were built and land transportation became the primary mode of moving people and goods on

Greenbank Store remains a community center, 2014. *Private collection.*

the island, the Greenbank store was moved away from the beach to what was then the primary road through the area, now Firehouse Road. In the '30s, when the main road was moved to its current location, a new store was built fronting the highway. The older store became an addition to the newer one and remains in use as a neighborhood restaurant and gathering place. Just as in the old days, the Greenbank store and post office are together. You walk through an interior door of the store into a room where you can check your mailbox and buy your stamps.

From Dairy to Berry Farm

Although he had never been a farmer and remained a city dweller until the end of his life, Philips in 1904 started his demonstration model dairy farm. Local laborers cleared and maintained land, constructed silos and storage buildings, tended stock and grew feed for the animals. The barns, completed in 1906, were among the largest in the region. The Greenbank School moved into one of the farm's buildings in 1912.

The farm prospered. By 1914, it had a herd of seventy-five registered Holstein-Friesians and successful production of milk and butter. In addition to dairy cattle, swine and horses were tended. The farm had a blacksmith shop, a milking barn, mechanical milking machines and a tractor. Everything was up to date and well-managed thanks to the professional dairy managers Philips hired.

But then disaster struck. A new bull brought to the farm infected the entire herd with tuberculosis. All the cattle had to be destroyed or moved off-island where the disease was eradicated in the next generation through specialized breeding. The last professional dairy manager left, and Philips's sons took over managing the farm. Other caretakers followed.

The grounds and buildings of the farm were decontaminated. Eventually, a few cows were brought back for local rather than commercial use. But the model dairy farm was no more.

The property turned over in the 1940s when John Molz, dreaming of loganberries, purchased 522 acres of fields and woodlands. Loganberries, a blackberry-raspberry hybrid, were popular for wine, liqueur, preserves and baking. Molz planted the first loganberries on his property in 1943. By 1950, the farm was producing 130 tons of berries a year. By 1970, nearly one hundred pickers gathered 160 tons of loganberries. Blackberries, grapes and currants also grew at the site, which became the largest loganberry farm in the United States and possibly the world and was widely known for the loganberry liqueur it produced.

In addition to the Greenbank berries and grapes, Molz had begun to grow wine grapes in eastern Washington for another venture, American Wine Company, which produced wines under the name Chateau Ste. Michelle. When Molz wanted to sell the farm, the parent company of Chateau Ste. Michelle winery, Stimson Lane, bought it in 1971.

People loved the sight of the loganberry vines flourishing in neat rows across the gentle hills. The red barns were beloved by islanders and tourists alike. It is said the barns became one of the most photographed structures on the island. The affection felt for this place would soon become a powerful force in the farm's future.

THREAT OF DEVELOPMENT

In 1995, the peaceful view of the loganberry farm was altered with a "For Sale" sign. Stimson Lane had decided to sell it for $2.8 million.

Fear and rumors erupted in the community. Resident Kristi O'Donnell remembers, "We all took for granted this place would always be here. But things aren't always what they seem to be. This became our opportunity to make a choice."

Michael Seraphinoff, who had worked on the loganberry farm and knew the land intimately, served on the board of the Whidbey Environmental Action Network (WEAN). He recalls that WEAN organized the first public meeting in the Save the Farm movement. Eighty people showed up at the Greenbank Clubhouse (then the Greenbank Progressive Club). Friends of Whidbey Island, another local preservation group, joined the movement as co-creators and colleagues. The battle to save the farm began, and it was urgent: developers were avidly eyeing the beautiful property, aware of the spectacular views. There was talk of four to five hundred houses being sited on the slopes of the farm.

Greenbank neighbors took advantage of an unusual Washington law written by state senator Mary Margaret Haugen that allowed the creation of publicly elected community councils to take over local land use planning within any county "only consisting of islands." Greenbank residents petitioned Island County to form such a group. They became the Greenbank

Community Council. Seven people were elected to the council, including O'Donnell as chair and Seraphinoff as vice-chair.

A great number of islanders responded to the group's call to save the farm. Local Greenbank orchardist and seaman Captain Kelly Sweeney

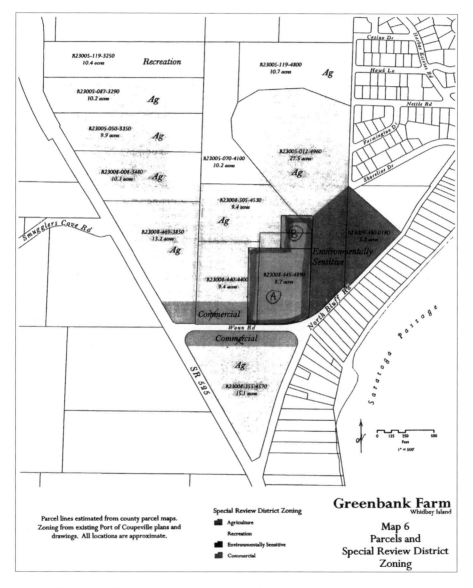

Map of Greenbank Farm, a complicated patchwork for a community treasure. *Courtesy of Whidbey Camano Land Trust.*

suggested that the Save the Farm group sponsor a letter-writing campaign, and hundreds of letters poured into county commissioners' offices, where issues that inspired even a dozen citizen letters were considered significant.

The council worked for the next two years until the law was stricken by the Washington Supreme Court. But by then, the immediate development of the farm had been averted.

Larry Kwarsick worked for Island County as Public Works director and manager of the Conservation Futures program. He recounts the myriad issues and many players who were involved: environmentalists, activists, residents, the Greenbank community, Island County, state elected officials, the Trust for Public Lands, the Nature Conservancy and the Port of Coupeville. The preservationists leveraged funds, secured loans, and negotiated deals among agencies that were willing to take risks and move forward together to preserve the farm.

The detailed work included negotiating easements for water access, clearing hazardous waste from earlier days on the farm and moving an old house from one landowner's property and storing it temporarily on another's

Sign at Greenbank Farm announcing and celebrating Conservation Easement, 2012. *Courtesy of Whidbey Camano Land Trust.*

until it could be moved permanently. People had to set aside their personal and official differences, and they did. Kwarsick considers his role in the saving of Greenbank farm as one of his top professional achievements. He recalls the complicated political, social, fiscal and environmental challenges that had to be overcome by creativity and cooperation.

In 1997, the farm was officially saved temporarily for public use. Island County purchased 308 wooded acres and the Nature Conservancy purchased 52. The Port of Coupeville purchased the operating farm. Each entity individually ensured public access. Island County filed a permanent Conservation Easement in December 2012, which will protect the historical features and conservation values of the land and keep the farm pastoral, regardless of who may own it in the future.

The Farm Today

That Greenbank Farm survived is a testament to the power of community activism. The heart of the farm, owned by the Port of Coupeville, is 151 acres that contain pasture, pond, barns and agricultural fields. The farm's fields, trails, wetlands and day-to-day operations are managed by a private nonprofit organization called the Greenbank Farm Management Group (GFMG) that also leases the ten-acre commercial area from the port to provide facilities for galleries, restaurants, shops, offices and community events, such as a farmers' market, festivals and celebrations.

The Washington State University Master Gardeners Program operates a demonstration garden on site. The Greenbank Garden Club installed and maintained other gardens around the historic buildings. Recreational opportunities include an off-leash area for exercising dogs, a variety of hiking trails and a playground.

The farm's agricultural land is certified as organic by the Washington Department of Agriculture so that all farming activity must comply with strict national standards. And there are still some loganberries growing on the farm—homage to the berry glory days and recognizing that loganberries are a living artifact of the farm's history. The area also supports community P-patches where people can grow produce for their own use, and another area where small-scale farmers can grow produce to sell locally. The farm operates a school to train new organic farmers. Pastureland is available for livestock, including horses, alpacas and sheep.

Most unusually, six local investors started a for-profit business in 2010 to farm energy in an area known as the Solar P-patch. Island Community Solar LLC leases the site from the Port of Coupeville. The company has installed solar panels to generate electrical power that can be sold back to the grid.

Judy Feldman, executive director of the GFMG, says, "We are a soil farm. And we are a farmer farm." In addition to training new farmers, the Greenbank Farm is making an intensive effort to restore soil depleted by logging, burning and the impact of crops that were not appropriate to the soil. Instead of animal manure and chemicals, the farmers use plants that fix nitrogen (convert atmospheric nitrogen into soil-enriching microorganisms) while they are alive and then, when plowed under, add rich organic matter to the soil. They are carefully planting what the soil can healthily bear. "We'll know we're there when what you want to grow, grows," says Feldman.

There is much to do for this beautiful old place and for the community that loves and cares for it. As novelist and poet Wendell Berry says:

> *Because a community is, by definition, placed, its success cannot be divided from the success of its place, its natural setting and surroundings: its soils, forests, grasslands, plants and animals, water, light and air. The two economies, the natural and the human, support each other. Each is the other's hope of a durable and livable life.*

6
Whidbey Institute

The Whidbey Institute rests on land—now called the Chinook Land—that has been shaped by people for purposes including heavy logging followed by farming. Today, the institute hosts restored forests, meadows and wetlands. Within that restorative environment, people come to understand that the quality of interaction between land and people shapes the human future.

As YOU TURN ONTO Old Pietila Road in South Whidbey's Maxwelton Valley, it's the trees that capture your attention. Stately forests of Douglas fir, red cedar and hemlock line both sides of the narrow pavement, anchored by delicate ferns and the mottled green leaves of the undergrowth. The distracting cacophony of daily life falls away, slowly at first, replaced by the sounds of nature interspersed with stillness. Dappled light streams through branches, splashing the narrow road in front of you. You are now on the Chinook Land, named to honor the native peoples who were first in the region and the largest type of salmon, now in decline.

The narrow road dips down for a time. A sign points toward the Legacy Forest and the Story House, a cozy place for small gatherings. Other paths branch off and lead to cabins—either restored buildings or new construction done in a rustic style. Nearly four miles of nature trails, including one section for which an interpretive guide is provided, invite hikers to walk throughout the beautiful property.

After about a quarter mile, the road climbs and quickly approaches a clearing. The fifteen-acre site was once the Pietila family farm. This was the

Sunrays stream through the magnificent trees within the Whidbey Institute. *Courtesy of Whidbey Institute and photographer Mary Jakubiak.*

Entrance to Thomas Berry Hall. *Courtesy of Whidbey Institute and photographer Mary Jakubiak.*

Doors open to the Great Hall, located within Thomas Berry Hall. *Courtesy of Whidbey Institute and photographer Mary Jakubiak.*

first parcel of what is now the one-hundred-acre Chinook Land, home to the present-day Whidbey Institute.

Thomas Berry Hall comes into view at the road's end. It was built in 1997 with a gift from Margaret Lloyd, a generous friend of the institute. Thomas Berry, for whom the hall is named, was a Catholic priest, cultural historian and inspirational scholar of the earth, ecology and the human spirit.

The building is simple and geometric, designed by local architect Ross Chapin in a traditional Northwest style. Artisans led by builder Greg Gilles constructed it. A small grove of alder that once stood here was cut and milled and has become the floor. A huge cedar stump, found adrift on the shores of another island, was hauled back to create the wide, welcoming doors, crafted locally by Kim Hoelting. Soaring windows are artfully framed in Douglas fir. Light pours into the great hall, the large main room of Thomas Berry Hall. It is an inspiring gathering place for conferences, programs, retreats, lectures and musical performances.

CREATING THE CHINOOK LAND

During the late nineteenth century, the Pietila family carved out their farm on logged-over land. Some sixty years later, Fritz and Vivienne Hull, anticipating the emergence of a new ecological age, purchased the old farm with a dream of creating, as Fritz describes it, "a small community of learners...who were somehow part of a transformational cultural shift."

Fritz writes in his unpublished memoir of seeing the farm for the first time: "I sensed that the land was drawing me to itself...it was speaking to me." In the following years, he "learned to expect the very land itself would guide us."

It was 1966, a time when the cultural fabric of American life was changing. Rachel Carson had published her now famous book, *Silent Spring*, in 1962 and awakened people to the importance of land and water resources. In 1964, Congress had passed the Wilderness Act, the first wilderness protection legislation in the world. It created the Land and Water Conservation Fund at the same time.

The abandoned Pietila farmhouse still stood when Fritz and Vivienne arrived, but it was in a state of ruin, with doors and windows gone and wallpaper hanging in shreds. A porch decorated with beach rocks, small arches and a curving stairway stretched across the front. The Pietilas had planted two massive white pine guardian trees, a common practice among Finnish people. A few steps away sat a handcrafted Finnish log sauna, an echo of the family's heritage. On their visits, Fritz and Vivienne chose to stay in a small cabin that was in better condition, located behind the barn.

It took an enormous amount of work to revive buildings and clean up the property. After a few years, the Hulls invited friends and neighbors to help complete the cleanup, create gardens and repair old buildings. They made the dilapidated old farmhouse livable once again. Fritz writes of the profound impact of working on and walking the land. He came to understand that "the heart and mind of our future would arise out of the land itself."

Together with people who had joined them to learn and work, Fritz and Vivienne created the Chinook Learning Center in 1972. It was a place for retreat and study, modeled after the Iona Community, a learning/serving community located in Scotland's Inner Hebrides on the Island of Iona. The Hulls had visited Iona two years before.

Fritz, an ordained Presbyterian minister, drew from the teachings of Thomas Berry and from his own deep connections to the land as he and Vivienne shaped the center's work. Berry's work integrates philosophy and

Fritz and Vivian Hull, 1970s. The old farmhouse is the building in the distance on the right side of the photo. *Courtesy of Whidbey Institute.*

science from diverse disciplines and links it with spirituality to create the Universe Story. His writings describe an entire universe that is a continually developing and creating community. His teachings urge mankind to learn from the universe and live with greater ecological responsibility.

Thus began a life's work, an effort that would inspire people far beyond Whidbey Island. Some would be drawn to live permanently on the island, influenced by Fritz and Vivienne's commitment to integrating nature and spirituality.

CHINOOK LAND

Forested land, regenerated from the devastation of earlier logging, surrounded the fifteen-acre site on which the Chinook Learning Center was located. It was "thick with ferns, great firs, hemlocks, and cedars" as Fritz tells it. Fearful of development nearby, Fritz and Vivienne began to seek opportunities to purchase the surrounding properties, thereby preserving the silent beauty of the land around them.

Over time, they added seven additional parcels, bringing the Chinook Land to a total of seventy-two acres. A neighbor gave them an old house, "Granny's House," in 1976. It was moved from its original spot to a newly purchased five-acre piece of land and was refurbished, and for a dozen years, it served as the site of a Sunday religious service that Fritz conducted.

In 1992, the Hulls successfully halted a proposed development next to them and arranged to purchase the land. The thirty-acre parcel had been logged several times. It became the Legacy Forest. It, too, eventually regenerated: trees reappeared along with native evergreen huckleberry, salal and other woodland plants. Beautiful mosses grow throughout. The addition of the Legacy Forest brought the Chinook Land to its present size.

Most of the Chinook Land has now been placed under the protection of the Whidbey Camano Land Trust to "preserve it as habitat for wildlife, native species of plants, water purity and for educational purposes." Five protected acres are wetlands, a designated critical habitat area. They contain a riparian zone, an interface between land and stream that plays an important role in soil conservation. Drainage flows both north and south from the two highest points in the wetlands area, into two salmon-bearing streams that eventually join nearby Maxwelton Creek as it flows through the Maxwelton watershed. (See Chapter 3.)

CREATION OF THE WHIDBEY INSTITUTE

By 1993, Fritz, Vivienne and others involved with the Chinook Learning Center began to wrestle with troubling changes in society. The laidback '70s with their heightened concern for the environment had evolved into an era of ambition, excess and explosive technological innovation. Specific to the work of the institute, a growing body of science more definitively linked ecological sustainability and the role of human behavior. There was, for example, scientific evidence that tied human activity to climate change. Challenged to rethink the focus of their work, the Hulls decided to invite others and return to Iona to reflect on future directions.

On Iona, the group came up with a plan for a new concept, one that maintained the core principles and values of the Chinook Learning Center but set far-reaching goals. The group aimed to cultivate and nurture deep personal development and a connection with community "on behalf of

The old farmhouse was restored in 2000. *Courtesy of Whidbey Institute and photographer Mary Jakubiak.*

Earth, Spirit and the Human Future." Two years later, the reenergized Chinook Learning Community became the Whidbey Institute.

Today, the Whidbey Institute is a multifaceted organization with a full-time staff, unique collaborative partners and an international presence and reach. Programs are year round. The old Pietila farmhouse, more fully restored in 2000 with a generous gift from local philanthropist Nancy Nordhoff, links past with present and provides a quiet setting for intimate gatherings and accommodations for overnight guests. It remains on its original site just down the slope from Thomas Berry Hall and is still anchored by the beautiful porch and stone steps. The old handcrafted Finnish sauna has been refurbished.

Other buildings provide housing for a resident caretaker and, for about half the year, a land apprentice, a young person who works with the institute's land coordinator. The apprentice learns sustainable and environmentally friendly gardening and management practices based on a respectful interaction with the land. She or he works with schoolchildren and a steadfast group of regular volunteers who come to help with planting, harvest and required maintenance.

The Westgarden and the Flower Garden sit just down the hill from the farmhouse. Most of the food grown in the Westgarden goes to Good Cheer,

Sunlight shines through the trees onto the labyrinth. *Courtesy of Whidbey Institute and photographer Mary Jakubiak.*

the local food bank, for distribution to South Whidbey families. The rest is prepared in the large commercial kitchen located in Thomas Berry Hall. It nourishes the staff, the volunteers and the numerous visitors to the institute.

Another nearby site, a small clearing surrounded by evergreens, is home to a labyrinth. A single, nonbranching and circular path is set on carefully tended ground. Small rocks, some carried back from Iona, line the walking space that leads to the center of the circle. People walk the labyrinth in quiet contemplation.

Nearby is the sanctuary. Designed by Ross Chapin and built by Kim Hoelting, with a financial gift from Judy Yeakel, it is thought by many to be the spiritual center of the land. Generous windows and skylights open to the surrounding forest. It is a place of quiet meditation and has a small library.

There are many opportunities for peaceful walks along trails that wind upward toward ridges, across wetlands, through forests thick with trees and into light-filled clearings. Resting spots abound. Some are along ridges that look out toward Puget Sound. Others are nestled among the trees; a small log or stump offers a place to perch and observe the rich life of the forest. Each provides a tranquil place to commune with nature.

LAND SHAPES WORK

There are many opportunities for interaction with the land. People who come to participate in programs often seek a chance to step back from a life that may feel overly demanding. They can be overheard to say, "As soon as I arrived, it felt like home." They discover what Fritz learned in 1966: the land calls out to them, infuses their spirit and, as reported by more than a few, changes lives.

"What makes this place so special?" is a question often posed to land coordinator Maggie Mahle. A former wilderness guide, she draws on her many experiences in beautiful places as she answers, "Beauty is a relationship. The land is responsive to human energy. This land is loved and cared for." She goes on to observe that some places don't generate the same energy or a feeling of life. In those places, she explains, "People may not have the same deep connection with the land."

"The land aligns us by its presence," says institute director Jerry Milhon. Listening to and caring for the land guides Jerry and his board of directors as they create programs that advance the mission and draw on the natural environment. They believe people who come will be "captivated by the land." Time on the land—engaging with others, walking the trails or sitting quietly under a tree—is part of learning. The total experience challenges the mind and refreshes the spirit while gracious hospitality and fresh, locally grown food nurtures the body.

Jerry tells of a recent lightning strike that hit one of the older, taller trees on the property, causing a fire that took more than a day to extinguish. It destroyed the tree, but in its place, he notes, new growth has created new energy, a continuation of life. He sees the natural process of regeneration as germane to the work of the institute and to the individual experiences of participants. Institute programs are designed to attract a broad audience, diverse in age and culture, and to shape future leaders and challenge current thinking.

The specter of climate change brought on by human assault on the world's resources goes to the heart of the institute's mission. Larry Daloz, one of the early founders and a former institute director and board member, takes on the challenge. He is organizing a continuing series of conferences that will, as he describes it, "build a core of leaders who have the requisite moral depth, shared commitment, compassionate resolve and strength of soul to sustain themselves and others through one of the most difficult transitions our species has ever faced." Over the past year, he has invited seventy-five of the most committed and effective climate leaders from the Northwest's Cascadia Bioregion to come

Participants in a Whidbey Institute program gather in the Great Hall, located in Thomas Berry Hall. *Courtesy of Whidbey Institute and photographer Mary Jakubiak.*

together at the institute for the first in a series of conferences on "Moral Power for Climate Action: Cultivating a Committed Core."

For the past three years, the institute has hosted a regional meeting of Bioneers, people who are part of a national movement concerned with the world's most pressing environmental and social problems. They look to the lessons of nature for solutions, drawing from the perspective of many disciplines. Bioneers of all ages come from many walks of life: farming, science, education, social justice advocacy, the health professions and others. They study and learn together in gatherings both large and small. Individual reflection and quiet walks amid tall trees nurture their learning.

Another institute initiative connects creative leaders whose work helps their respective communities thrive. These innovative community leaders are invited from Whidbey Island and communities across Washington State. They come to share ideas and experiences. Participants tell about their work through video storytelling and conversation—at presentations, over meals and during walks in the woods.

The first-year participants described innovative gardening and food distribution programs that reduced, with the goal of eliminating, hunger in their respective communities. This past year, participants explored effective ways to nurture and sustain local economies. Next year, participants will focus on promoting health and healthy communities.

THE LAND AS LEGACY

The Chinook Land is the unifying force for the work of the Whidbey Institute. "The land demands that the organization stay coherent," said Larry Daloz as he talks of the future. "As long as the institute stays involved with work that truly matters, work that is connected to the land, it will persist."

The two white pine trees, planted by the Pietila family next to their porch more than one hundred years ago, were beloved by many. This past year, they finally reached the ends of their lives. Jerry and others spent time with the trees and talked among themselves about what should be done.

Ultimately, the beautiful trees had to be taken down. But before that happened, the two old pines were honored in a ceremony that recognized their longevity and presence as friends, guardians and symbols of home and family. The wood from the trees will be used to generate new chairs, tables, benches and bowls crafted by local artists.

These two white pines guarded the old farmhouse for over one hundred years. In 2013, they reached the end of their lives and were recognized and celebrated for their longevity before they were taken down. *Courtesy of Whidbey Institute and photographer Mary Jakubiak.*

Regeneration is a powerful part of legacy. When the land is respected and cherished, it will thrive and continue to guide, teach and touch the spirit of generations to come. That is the signature lesson of the Whidbey Institute. People shape the land, but it is the quality of interaction with the land that ultimately shapes the future.

7

Deception Pass State Park

*D*ramatic. Breathtaking. Mysterious and misty. Most people find it beyond words and choose to take pictures instead. At the north end of Whidbey Island, this park, with its remarkable history and iconic bridge, is an exceptional place that stirs the imagination and quiets the soul.

"THE U.S. MILITARY IS the reason that we have Deception Pass Park," explained park manager Jack Hartt as he leaned back in his chair. "President Andrew Johnson issued an executive order in 1866 that set aside 1,700 acres at Deception Pass for a military reservation. That action kept those prime lands off-limits forever. In 1922, the federal government offered that land to Washington State for a park."

One of the first state parks, Deception Pass languished quietly for years. When the Washington State legislature authorized state parks in 1913, it provided no money for facilities. That had to wait until 1933, when the Civilian Conservation Corps (CCC), a federal work relief program, began constructing buildings, roads and campgrounds there. A New Deal agency, the Public Works Administration (PWA), funded a long-sought bridge in 1935. It linked Whidbey and Fidalgo Islands and joined the two main sections of the park. From its original 1,700 acres, the park today has grown to more than 4,100 acres following many additions. "Today," says Hartt, "it's the most visited Washington State Park. Some two million people come each year."

What is it about this somewhat out-of-the-way place that attracts so many people? Spectacular scenery? Majestic cliffs over the dramatic turbulence of

Deception Pass Bridge. *Courtesy of John Evans, www.on-scenic-routes.com.*

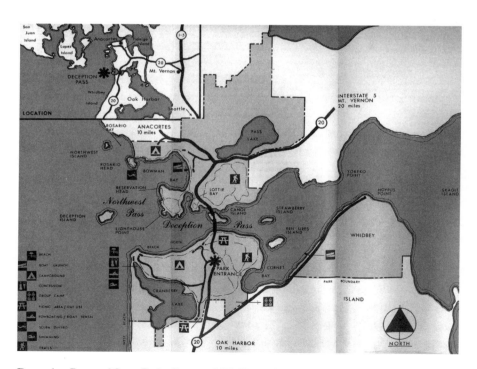

Deception Pass and State Park. *Courtesy of Washington State Parks.*

water flowing through the pass? The opportunity to face the wind straight across the Pacific Ocean and feel its force? Maybe it's the chance to see migrating whales or varieties of seabirds. Perhaps it's the irony that its military potential helped protect this amazing place. Or is it because it spans two counties and is filled with extraordinary natural and human history? What is it about Deception Pass?

VIEW FROM THE BRIDGE

On a clear day, the view from the bridge is extraordinary. To the west, you look past Deception Island toward the San Juan Islands, Victoria, British Columbia and the Pacific Ocean and then down to the Olympic Peninsula near Port Angeles. South are beaches and forests of Whidbey. To the east are small islands (Strawberry, Ben Ure, Kiket), Hoypus Point, and the mainland. Turning north, you see the smooth rock faces of Pass, Canoe and Fidalgo Islands.

Carved by glaciers—perhaps also helped by an earthquake fault or water flow under glaciers—Deception Pass State Park includes part of Whidbey and Fidalgo Islands along with a cluster of smaller islands in the fast-moving waters of the pass. Rugged, steep cliffs and sharp edges of land create natural barriers and divert tides flowing between the Strait of Juan de Fuca and the Saratoga Passage.

On the steep slopes of the islands are markedly different vegetations. The north-facing slopes of Whidbey Island are cooler and moister, completely covered with trees, primarily Douglas fir. The drier and warmer south-facing slopes of Fidalgo are rocky. Tucked into crevices are grasses, rose, stunted Douglas fir and madrone. This dramatic contrast in adjoining places is unusual in western Washington. It gives reason to pause and take in the scenery.

Boats of many sizes navigate the pass waters regularly, but tidal flow through the pass can be extremely rough and challenge even experienced boaters. Oceanographer Richard Strickland described it this way: "The massive (twice daily) tidal ebb and flood currents, unobstructed as they traverse the Strait of Juan de Fuca to and from the Pacific Ocean, shoot through the narrow, rough defile of Deception Pass like a fire hose."

In fact, the waters of Deception Pass contain the fastest, trickiest and most dangerous currents of Puget Sound. At the times of the strongest currents, an estimated two million cubic feet of water pour through the pass every second, eight times greater than the Columbia River and more

Trees in Deception Pass State Park. *Courtesy of Whidbey Camano Land Trust and photographer Mark Sheehan.*

than fifty times the average flow of all rivers emptying into the sound. By constantly scouring the cliffs, these currents move sediments emptying into the Saratoga Passage from the nearby Skagit River. Without those forceful currents, perhaps Whidbey wouldn't be an island today.

HUMAN CONNECTION

Long before there was a Washington Territory, tribal people recognized the beauty and honored the spirit of Deception Pass's waters and lands. They navigated their canoes through the waters with legendary skill for generations. They beached their canoes to fish and harvest edible plants. The land sheltered, fed and inspired them. Within the park boundaries are tributes to their stories of relationship with the land and water. The place was, and is, sacred for them.

White explorers looking for convenient ways to enter a protected inland passage felt deceived by the topography, thinking it was a bay and not a through-route. For decades, North Whidbey Island settlers navigated the turbulent waters on supply runs. Illegal clandestine operations found

Jack Hartt, Deception Pass Park manager, holding a decorative canoe paddle given to him by the Samish tribe to honor how he cares for the land. *Courtesy of Jack Hartt.*

the misty, foggy small islands helpful to shelter their contraband work.

The first white explorers credited with seeing Deception Pass were led by Juan de Fuca, a Greek mariner employed by the Spanish crown during the late sixteenth century. Two centuries later, George Vancouver, exploring for

England, sailed around Puget Sound and up the east side of Whidbey Island. As he often did, Vancouver sent out a small boat, captained by his chief navigator, Joseph Whidbey, to survey the coastline. They traveled up the east side to what they thought was the north end of Saratoga Passage and then back down and around to explore the west side. In the process, Whidbey and crew realized that the turbulent waters were a pass and that the land they were exploring was actually an island. Vancouver named the island for his chief navigator. Annoyed at or respectful of the land's appearance, Vancouver called the waterway Deception Pass.

In the decades-long process of exploring western Washington, Europeans connected with many tribes, sharing food, tools and more. Those tribes, in turn, continued the trade with others. Vancouver's diary recounts stories of meeting native tribes who were astonished at the white color of the Europeans' skin. Yet the native people had tools and manufactured items such as buttons that clearly demonstrated earlier trade between Europeans and native tribes. As is now well known, native people contracted many diseases from whites that decimated their population.

A wave of white settlers came in the mid-nineteenth century as part of the vast migrations from Europe and from east of the Mississippi River in the United States. With local native populations a fraction of their earlier size, the new settlers had little competition for the land and natural resources they coveted. They settled in and began to build their lives on Whidbey.

DEVELOPING ECONOMY

Many whites who settled on Whidbey Island farmed and fished. They built a growing community, most of it centered in Coupeville. To the north, a small but vibrant agricultural settlement was taking shape around Oak Harbor. People recognized that Deception Pass was the shortest distance to another island with the mainland close by. By 1900, there was growing interest in a bridge across the pass. It would take more than three decades for the bridge to become reality. In the meantime, Whidbey Island was connected to the larger Puget Sound community by boat, run by private ferry companies.

The commercial route from Deception Pass was served by the Deception Pass Ferry Company, which was owned by a spunky, hardworking Norwegian woman, Berte Olsen, and her husband, Augie. Berte was the first female

Berte Olsen, owner of the Deception Pass Ferry Company. *Courtesy of Jill Johnson.*

ferry captain in Puget Sound. The company's two ferry runs served Whidbey, Fidalgo and Camano Islands.

The Olsens operated one of many private ferry businesses around Puget Sound for more than fifty years. Thousands of boats moved people, supplies, livestock, agriculture, machinery and timber—everything needed to build and serve the new settlements. Virtually all settlements had piers or floats to receive the boats. This Mosquito Fleet—so named because its numbers and activity resembled a swarm of mosquitoes—was the vital link to the outside, larger community. The ferries, mostly wood-fueled steamers, provided the principal transport in Puget Sound until the mid-1930s.

THE BRIDGE

On Whidbey Island, the decades-long goal of a bridge over Deception Pass gained momentum. About 1900, an early Oak Harbor settler, Captain

Workers prepare for the construction of the Deception Pass Bridge. *Courtesy of Island County Historical Society.*

George Morse, envisioned such a bridge. As a new representative to the state legislature in 1907, he secured an appropriation of $20,000 to build one. Quite quickly, his dream faded as the legislature rescinded the appropriation. Yet in 1929, with intense lobbying by North Whidbey citizens, the legislature passed a bill to build the bridge. Berte Olsen lobbied hard for Governor Roland Hartley to veto the bill. When an effort to override the veto failed, Berte rejoiced.

Much earlier, North Whidbey residents had organized the Deception Pass Bridge Association to get the bridge built. In 1918, they promoted it as necessary for the war effort, and state legislators wrote an appeal to Congress citing its military importance. With the veto of the 1929 bill, the association was reenergized and worked to generate community interest in building the bridge. Picnics at Cranberry Lake in the park were annual events to organize community enthusiasm for the project.

In 1933, the Washington legislature finally approved a bill to construct the bridge, and Governor Clarence D. Martin signed it into law. Construction of the bridge was a Great Depression public works project funded by the Federal Emergency Relief Administration (FERA) and the Works Progress Administration (WPA) as well as by Island County.

Depression Memories

The Great Depression hit many on Whidbey Island hard, but others recalled that their lives were already difficult. Some female teachers who had families went home because there was no money to pay them. Jobs were scarce and money scarcer. Grocery stores ran tabs for farmers, who paid their bills annually. While islanders certainly made do with less than they had during the 1920s, the stories handed down tell of a sense of community where neighbors helped one another survive.

There were always venison and fish, so most people ate regularly. Up and down the island, most people continued to live simply, and they all seemed to be in the same situation. Even so, the years of little money and few prospects eventually wore spirits down. People started to look for ways to build and broaden the economy. They wanted jobs.

For North Whidbey residents, news that the bridge was authorized cheered them. Besides access, the bridge would mean jobs. Already, the CCC was employing some two hundred young men—mostly from out of state— to build park facilities. Their presence sparked youthful adventures, and many parents kept their daughters under close watch. Now there would also be work on the bridge.

The Washington State Highway Department was one of the primary sources of Depression-era relief. Under state highway director Lacey Van Buren Murrow, the Deception Pass Bridge was constructed in less than a year. This engineering marvel was dedicated and opened in 1935. It gracefully links three land masses and makes Deception Pass State Park much easier to access. The bridge dramatically opened up Whidbey Island, and the area began to grow and change pretty rapidly.

In the late '30s, the U.S. Navy began to look at North Whidbey as a possible seaplane base for the PBY, a patrol bomber built by Catalina Aircraft. The logical place for that base was on the peninsula that jutted out into Crescent Harbor in Oak Harbor. With the bridge over Deception Pass, the navy also considered placing a second, larger base in Clover Valley, just a few miles south of Deception Pass State Park. Small, rural communities around the small city of Oak Harbor looked appealing as a location for a training base. After the attack on Pearl Harbor and U.S. entry into World War II, the timetable sped up to establish a naval air station west of Seattle. The navy chose Oak Harbor.

That selection effectively ended the Depression for North Whidbey. Almost immediately, hundreds of jobs became available. Many people involved in military construction or service moved to Whidbey Island, fell in love with the place and decided to live here permanently someday.

THE PARK GROWS

Whidbey's population increased. More people visited the Deception Pass State Park to camp, hold picnics and generally enjoy all the experiences it offered. The park became the site of precious family memories, shared by generations.

With several significant additions, this much-loved park has nearly tripled in size. The small islands in Deception Pass, Hoypus Hill and Hoypus Point on Whidbey, as well as the Pass Lake area on Fidalgo Island are now formally part of the park. In addition, the park manages nearby Dugualla State Park as a satellite.

Besides the many natural and historical treasures, the park offers important interpretive resources. Visitors can learn about the park's diverse, remarkable nature and its impressive history. While hiking, they can explore their way through old-growth forests that come right down to the water's edge or see habitat that hosts many kinds of wildlife, including the unusual and intriguing Townsends big-eared bats.

The most recent addition to the park is a ninety-four-acre island just east of the pass. Kiket Island is a cameo of the park's history and potential. Tribal land until just before the Great Depression, then privately owned and finally bought by the park in 2010, it is now jointly managed by the Washington State Parks system and the Swinomish tribe. The shared management goal is to make the area accessible in a way that minimizes human impact on this pristine land. It's about respecting this place, the land and its full natural heritage.

Majestic and Much More

A rich history, extraordinary natural assets and a past woven into the present. There's the indescribable joy of connecting with nature—on land and at the water's edge. And there's more.

Deception Pass, in common with all eight state parks on Whidbey Island, evokes something more, something linked to the essence of democracy. Echoing Teddy Roosevelt's comments at Yellowstone National Park in 1903, this park preserves a "track of veritable wonderland made accessible to all

Deception Pass Bridge today. *Courtesy of Walter Siegmund.*

visitors." By protecting and caring for this exceptional place as a public park, we ensure that all people, not just the wealthy, can enjoy nature's extraordinary places.

Protecting and caring for Deception Pass also requires that we work together. The land is what we have in common. This Earth is home to us all, a shared treasure. Appreciating and caring for our home depends on all of us.

8
Dugualla Bay

In 2009, the Whidbey Camano Land Trust concluded a long and complicated process to purchase land on the Saratoga Passage across from the Skagit River. Work began immediately to study how to restore the area for salmon and other wildlife. In doing so, community groups came face-to-face with a legacy of decades of different uses of this beautiful, open land. Restoring Dugualla Bay challenges people to face the aftermath of generations of short-term thinking about land use.

PAT POWELL, EXECUTIVE DIRECTOR of the Whidbey Camano Land Trust, can tell you that restoration is tough.

"The amount of time and energy and work that we have put into Dugualla is enormous," she asserts. "It is *much* easier to protect intact habitat and prevent problems than to try to solve them after the fact."

Powell has guided this project since learning in a phone call in early 2006 that property in Dugualla Bay was soon to be offered for sale by its Ducken family heirs. The caller expressed concern that the property would be sold, more houses would be built and the end result would jeopardize the neighborhood and environment. Powell knew that Dugualla Bay was a high priority for the scientists working to revitalize the threatened and endangered salmon population in Puget Sound. Perhaps the threat to the property could mobilize the community to do some long-term good for people and wildlife in the area.

From the initial call through purchasing the land and now working to restore healthy habitat, Powell and the land trust have connected with many cultures and attitudes that have shaped North Whidbey.

Dugualla's story illustrates how community priorities clash. And it shows how many people can find common ground in the process of protecting land and natural resources.

FARMS, JETS AND SALMON

From a car, you first see Dugualla Valley from the crest of a hill on the north or south sides. Forest-lined Highway 20 enters into the dramatic sweep of open space filled with cattle, row crops and views of water on the east and west sides. The inviting saucer bottom of the valley provides a sense of calm as you drink in the scenic vista from above and then drive down into the valley itself. Distant mountains provide a backdrop to the scene. In front of you are various details—squares of agriculture, a roadside produce stand and small roads going off the highway, winding out of sight to neighborhoods and small farms.

Overhead, U.S. Navy aircraft streak past, heading out to mission targets hundreds of miles away. After completing their training missions, jets and pilots head back and then circle and slow to land on Ault Field. This airstrip, part of the Naval Air Station Whidbey Island (NASWI), supports pilots learning to fly specialized combat jets. Flight paths cross over farmland with crops and cattle, wetlands, neighborhoods and the dike that keeps the salt water from the reclaimed farmland. Behind each airborne jet is a wide, nearly invisible ribbon of exhaust that drifts slowly to the land, settling on livestock, growing plants, and buildings. On a clear evening, silhouettes of the jets against the setting sun evoke memories for many veterans who now live in Dugualla. They're neighbors to farming families with a long history of raising crops on Whidbey.

Just three miles south of Deception Pass, this narrow section of Whidbey Island slopes gently and indents noticeably on the east, forming Dugualla Bay. Here for millennia, juvenile salmon, newly adapted to salt water, arrived following their first perilous journey. They would hatch in the Skagit River, travel as tiny fish from fresh to salt water, adapting along the way. As the Skagit River empties into the Saratoga Passage, the forceful river currents push them toward Dugualla. Then as now, they needed rest, food and time to grow before they head out to sea.

An estuary is the ideal place for juvenile salmon to prepare for their major journey to the ocean. Estuaries are the brackish zones where salt and fresh water mix. Constantly refreshed and nourished by tides and currents, they are some of the most outstanding and productive ecosystems for biodiversity in the world. In Dugualla Bay is one such ideal pocket estuary that juvenile salmon have always used.

There, abundant eelgrass helped create beds and meadows for various marine species. Juvenile salmon found shelter and food within the waving underwater grasses. After a few months, the salmon were strong enough to head to the ocean where they would mature. Eventually, they would make their way back into the Saratoga Passage and up the Skagit River to spawn. This natural process developed and supported a huge population of salmon, including Chinook salmon. Dugualla Bay was a vital part of the system.

For many centuries, native tribes roamed the Puget Sound and camped on North Whidbey to fish and gather local plants for food. Traveling by canoe from the mainland to the islands in the area, these people ate well, spent time working wood and creating beautiful baskets, and generally enjoyed a peaceful existence. In Dugualla Valley, they cultivated food plants and established campsites along the bay, always careful to be back from the area that flooded regularly with the tides. Their impact on the land was minimal, and the valley blossomed around them.

In 1792, their generally serene life ended with the arrival of white explorers first led by Captain George Vancouver. The new arrivals noticed the beauty of the island and met many native people on their journey through the area. That exploratory journey effectively introduced Whidbey Island to the world.

For the native people, it was disastrous. In just a few decades, more than half would die from disease transmitted by white explorers. For those who remained, their way of life was gone forever. But for the white explorers and later settlers, the discovery of Whidbey Island provided another opportunity to expand their settlements in the Puget Sound region.

CHANGES WITH WHITE SETTLEMENT

By the mid-nineteenth century, industrious and enterprising people from the eastern and midwestern United States began to travel to what is now Oregon and Washington to establish farms and businesses. Immigrants from several European countries also took their chances in this new land. The Irish, already displaced by the Great Famine and their growing protest of the English presence in Ireland, heard Whidbey Island described as much like "home." They were among the first to settle in the area of present-day Oak Harbor. The Irish farmed, fished, built businesses and established a strong community sense of place. Later immigrant groups to North Whidbey included Scandinavians and many Dutch who settled in the Dugualla area. They established dairy farms and grew many specialty crops.

Many of these new settlers had responded to enthusiastic promotions of opportunities to farm on Whidbey Island. Land available for farming had previously been forest filled with great conifers. These forests were cut down on a large scale using steam mechanization in the 1880s. The logged parcels were inexpensive and looked appealing. From promotional brochures, new settlers envisioned abundant harvests and economic opportunities. After all, the promoters assured them that land productive enough to grow very tall trees would definitely be able to grow crops, enough for both home consumption and sale to others.

Reality was different. Most crops familiar to the settlers didn't thrive, and native plants were unproductive as crops. The soils that supported forests were not necessarily good for farming. For most settlers, farming fed their families but definitely did not create financial stability. An exception was an area of Dugualla Valley known as Clover Valley.

The rich soil of Clover Valley was a loamy and fertile prairie. To the newly arrived settlers it practically begged to become productive farmland. Not much higher than sea level, Clover Valley had been flooded historically by tidal action via Dugualla Bay. When the Dutch arrived in the late nineteenth century, they brought knowledge of how to work with the sea beside them. Clover Valley harvests were abundant. In fact, for a few years in the twentieth century, Clover Valley set national records for the number of bushels of wheat per acre that it produced.

THE DIKES

To make new farmland, it was critical to separate low-lying areas from the sea and regulate saltwater flooding. That required dikes. People built them privately and even established group dike systems when they saw a need. In 1889, the first Washington State legislature provided for a variety of special purpose districts, including diking and drainage districts.

These districts were a kind of government unit with defined boundaries, a governance structure and designated sources of funding. Generally, counties establish special purpose districts to meet a specific need of the community. To help create and enlarge farmable areas, Island County established diking districts in the early twentieth century. (Today, Island County has twenty-one special purpose districts to manage services including water, sewer, parks, fire, hospitals and dikes. The county has a fiduciary role limited to collecting taxes and disbursing funds.) In the Dugualla area about 1918, Island County Diking District #3 built a wide, earthen and rock wall across the bay to create farmland.

Opinions differ as to how good that farmland was, but the dikes definitely changed the natural processes on which the salmon depend. What benefitted livestock and row crops decimated salmon habitat. As long as the human population remained small, the negative effect on salmon wasn't noticed. But as more settlers came and developed the area, things changed. And the population continued to grow in the area north of Oak Harbor.

Micro-Communities

At least a dozen intersections in North Whidbey became social gathering places for the community in the early twentieth century. Cornet Bay, Watson's Corner, Crescent Harbor, Strawberry Point and Swantown are among the colorful names of places where people connected with their friends and relatives. Except to attend school or visit a post office, most people didn't venture too far from home. Isolated much of the time, people in these tucked away micro-communities were cautious about those that they didn't know. The Ducken family lived in one such small community on Dugualla Bay.

Joseph Cornelius Ducken stopped on Whidbey Island about 1898 en route from South Dakota to the gold fields in Alaska. He liked what he saw and returned seven years later to stay. He brought his wife, Bella, to Dugualla Bay where they settled, raised their family and became landowners. Joseph's brother Ben also visited and bought land in the area. Every month, the brothers traveled to La Conner for supplies.

Joseph's grandson Joe tells stories of his grandfather's many business efforts over a decade: a sawmill to make lumber, boat building and repair, commercial fishing and raising cattle and chickens. His grandfather served as a county commissioner in the 1920s. Over time, he acquired hundreds of acres of North Whidbey land. When Joseph Cornelius died, his sons logged some of that property south of the dike and developed

Dugualla Bay shoreline. *Courtesy of Whidbey Camano Land Trust and photographer Cheryl Lowe.*

the Dugualla Bay Heights area for residences. About 1962, they began to sell those building lots. At the water's edge and sloping up the hill, a neighborhood came into being.

Other families moved to North Whidbey in the early twentieth century to find homes and make lives. Descendants of many still live on original holdings. Names such as Muzzall, Christensen, and Frostad walk us through North Whidbey history. Farming was the mainstay for most. Dairy, livestock, specialty crops, and grain were all part of the essential agriculture.

Oak Harbor, initially settled in the 1850s by Irish, followed by Scandinavians and then Dutch immigrants, was incorporated in 1915 and became the big city in the area, even though its population was less than five hundred in the 1930s. It was there, in the city, that the Great Depression seemed to hit harder than on the farms. To the open lands outside Oak Harbor came refugees from the Dust Bowl thrilled to see the water all around Whidbey. Many thrived in the area north of Oak Harbor, farming and supporting one another during the Depression.

CHANGE WITH THE NAVY

In early 1941, the U.S. Navy began to look for a place well west of Sand Point Naval Air Station on Lake Washington to refuel and rearm Catalina Flying Boats. Defense of Puget Sound was the goal, and officers looked as far west as the Olympic Peninsula. They chose Forbes Point on Crescent Harbor, part of Oak Harbor, and they bought the land from descendants of Samuel Maylor, an early Oak Harbor settler. Very soon, construction workers began building roads, laying utility lines, and pouring concrete to build the seaplane base.

By November, the navy decided that Whidbey would also be ideal for an airfield. Immediately after the attack on Pearl Harbor, surveyors began marking a 4,300-acre area northwest of Oak Harbor, in the Clover Valley of Dugualla. The place seemed ideal—flat, approachable by aircraft from almost any direction and far enough from populated areas for practice bombing. Twenty farmers—some more willing than others—sold their property to the navy. Some property was even taken via eminent domain. Within a year, the Naval Air Station was commissioned. In 1943, the airfield was named for William Ault, who went missing-in-action at the Battle of the Coral Sea in 1942.

The population of Oak Harbor grew, doubling every decade from the 1940s through the '60s. With that population came more construction, hence more businesses, jobs and schools. Oak Harbor remained the largest city on Whidbey. The areas north, including Dugualla, also grew.

Some of the changes brought by the navy were troubling. Rich, productive farmland became the landing strip for the airfield, housing and office buildings on the base and even a golf course. For many of the farmers, there was both patriotism and bitterness. Ron Muzzall estimates that the navy eliminated some 60 to 70 percent of all agricultural land on North Whidbey. Still, the navy provided jobs, something people were hungry for at the end of the Depression and again at the end of World War II.

Population, city size, suburban-type development, roads, traffic, construction and pollution all increased on North Whidbey, including in Dugualla Valley. Not slowly or subtly, the land was changing.

SALMON PRIORITY

By 1977, people began to notice a significant decrease in the number of salmon caught in Puget Sound. Some efforts began to address the problem, but it became clear that a piecemeal approach was not effective. In the 1990s, the federal government declared more than a dozen populations of Puget Sound salmon threatened or endangered.

Research identified the loss and destruction of habitat as primary factors causing the precipitous decline in salmon. The simple solution was to restore salmon habitat. A quick look at the map of the Skagit River basin shows how important Dugualla Bay is for salmon, and restoring the estuarine environment in that location became a priority to help the salmon population recover.

But Dugualla Bay had changed quite a bit since the first half of the century. There were many houses and roads in the valley. The dike had reduced the area where salmon could find refuge and feed. In the Dugualla Heights neighborhood, a historic estuarine lagoon had been altered dramatically. The open tidal connection was gone there, and all that remained was a single, small drainage pipe that was now clogged with mussels. Salmon were on their own once they left the Skagit River.

The Ducken family land to be put on sale in 2006 was right in the middle of all the salmon priority coast land. The challenge was twofold: to protect from development the area that could be restored and then to restore the land, as possible, to help bring back the salmon.

When Powell received the call, she got busy immediately. She contacted John Ducken, the family's spokesman, and offered the land trust as a possible buyer. A three-year process began—filled with negotiating, fundraising and community outreach—to buy the land and protect it from development. Only then would it be possible to restore habitat for salmon and wildlife. Many shorebirds and waterfowl—including snow geese, western sandpiper, dunlin and several duck species—migrate through the Dugualla area. They, too, need places to rest and feed.

The Dugualla Bay project includes four properties. Together they comprise 152 acres with more than 4,500 feet of Dugualla Bay shoreline, adjacent to four miles of public coastal beaches. Among the properties is the historic estuarine lagoon in the Dugualla Heights neighborhood. The land trust worked with the local homeowners' association to put a conservation easement on the lagoon area and set the stage for restoring it. Except for one acre, all the properties were purchased from the Ducken family. The land ultimately purchased was valued at $2.3 million.

The land trust secured grants from many different agencies to pay for the land. Money came from the Washington State Salmon Recovery Funding Board (SRFB), the Island County Conservation Futures Fund, the Doris Duke Charitable Foundation's Northwest Wildlife Initiative and other sources, including private donations to the land trust. The Ducken family also helped with a generous donation of land.

AN AMBITIOUS PLAN

In 2010, just a month after the last purchase papers were signed, the land trust began a feasibility study about restoration. Funded by the SRFB, the study examined options and shared them with the community. Key places for restoration were the neighborhood lagoon and land just east of Dike Road, part of a historic estuary complex.

The land trust developed a plan to restore juvenile salmon rearing habitat in a degraded near-shore ecosystem in the lagoon in the Dugualla Heights neighborhood. It includes replacing a culvert with an open tidal channel and tide gate as well as restoring the lagoon topography to a more natural condition. That requires removing invasive plants and planting native species

Dugualla Heights Lagoon. *Courtesy of Whidbey Camano Land Trust and photographer Cheryl Lowe.*

to create high marsh and a more natural, native environment of shrubs and trees. In addition, the plan is to bring a portion of a small, natural stream into daylight.

The process continues slowly. Many people and groups are involved: the U.S. Corps of Engineers, Washington Department of Natural Resources Washington State University Beachwatchers, the Washington State Department of Fish and Wildlife, the Washington State Department of Ecology Water Resources Inventory Area #6, Island County, the National Recreation and Conservation Service, Naval Air Station Whidbey Island, Diking District #3 and the Dugualla Heights community. They all have opinions and preferences. Federal, state and local government, as well as native tribes, scientists and citizen-scientists and local homeowners grapple with the complexity of it all. Restoration is always a work in progress.

U.S. NAVY INTEREST

Tom Slocum, the project engineer working with the land trust, explains why the U.S. Navy is interested in this work. "They want to avoid Canada geese. They're a hazard to the pilots and the jets. The existing landscape, with all the pastureland, really attracts the geese. So restoration there would help with the navy's focus on safety—pilots and citizens."

Land restoration includes cleanup. The land around Ault Field experienced substantial groundwater contamination over the decades of aircraft use and maintenance. The U.S. Environmental Protection Agency (EPA) identified the Dugualla area near the airfield as a federal Superfund site due to waste from aircraft maintenance and fuel dumping. The cleanup program spanned several years with periodic monitoring continuing. Since 1990, the Naval Air Station has sponsored and expanded recycling efforts on base that have won multiple awards.

TOUGH WORK

Restoration is both mechanical and emotional. Specific, necessary changes are needed to protect and restore the environment. There are long-held beliefs that need to change as well.

All restoration projects take time. Some things can't be hurried, and it's difficult to wait. In Dugualla, a key part of restoring salmon habitat has to do with water—where it is, how clean it is, what temperature it is. Good salmon habitat includes trees that provide shade canopy over the water. It takes some fifty years for cedar trees to grow large enough to provide that canopy. Forests have been gone a long time from Dugualla Bay. Sapling trees, planted by many volunteers, will grow, but slowly. We must be patient.

Restoration also attempts to go back in time, which is impossible. The best we can do is habitat improvement. Doing so requires accepting, and even embracing, change, which we do reluctantly. Restoration projects inevitably include compromises among competing land uses. Many people like the theoretical idea of restoration but only as long as it doesn't affect their personal interests.

Tom Slocum reflected on the complex natural habitat that is the Whidbey Island coastline and how decisions for development have changed the land: "There's no doubt that waterfront property is appealing and valuable. Probably a lot of building done in the past wouldn't be allowed today, now that we know more. But it's happened, and so we work with it."

Our country has a strong tradition of private property rights that often trumps other land use considerations. Projects such as the Dugualla Bay restoration challenge us to think about our attitudes and beliefs as well as effects and lessons learned.

9

Lagoon Point

Before intensive development, Lagoon Point was largely a saltwater marsh. Its beach was renowned for fine fishing—a place where salmon could be hooked from land as the movement of the water brought them in close to shore. Now nearly five hundred homes cluster along the shoreline of Admiralty Inlet, around a man-made lake, up on a two-hundred-foot bluff and on two canals carved out for backyard boat moorage and easy access to the sea. It couldn't happen today, but now what can we do?

RECORDS IN THE ISLAND County Auditor's office confirm that Calvin Philips, the founder of Greenbank, sold 206 acres at Lagoon Point to the U.S. government in June 1909.

Janet Ferguson, who grew up at Lagoon Point from the early 1950s, recalls evidence of U.S. Navy presence at Lagoon Point in the form of old wells and foundations for recreational cabins for World War I–era officers. In 1929, the government sold the land to C.W. Major and I. Barrett for $2,500.

Originally platted in 1950, Lagoon Point became a small residential community of modest homes and fishing cabins. Most homes were on the lowland near the water, but some were built up on the bluff overlooking Admiralty Inlet. The developer created a little lake and used the fill for the foundation for homes around it. People could ford a creek over to hike in the saltwater marsh. They could fish off the beach, or use small "kicker boats" that didn't require a boat launch to get farther out into the water. This practice required calm waters and some expertise, but it was relatively common at Lagoon Point.

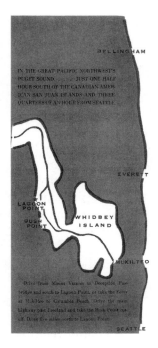

IN TODAY'S WORLD, MOST PEOPLE HAVE TO MAKE A CHOICE OF LIVING IN AN URBAN OR RURAL SETTING, ALTHOUGH BOTH HAVE THEIR SPECIAL BENEFITS. BUT NOW, YOU CAN HAVE THE BEST OF BOTH WORLDS . . . AT LAGOON POINT.

LAGOON POINT WATERFRONT HOMESITES BEGIN AT $9500*. FOR FURTHER INFORMATION ON THIS IDEAL WATERFRONT PROPERTY PLEASE CONTACT . . .
*PRICE IS SUBJECT TO CHANGE.

WASHINGTON STATES FINEST
WATERFRONT

LAGOON POINT

ON WHIDBEY ISLAND

Brochure advertising canal development at Lagoon Point. *Private collection.*

In 1969, a consortium called Lagoon Point Associates applied to Island County to construct new divisions in Lagoon Point's large saltwater marsh. To make it more attractive, the developers proposed dredging two canals along which residences could be built. These houses would have the highly desirable amenities of private docks and boat moorage. The developers would also dredge the small creek to make it navigable, using an enlarged lagoon as the basis for a boat turn-around area for the residents' vessels. To protect the newly navigable waterway from heavy windstorms common to the area, they would construct a jetty out into Admiralty Inlet.

These developments would significantly enlarge the small community with many new residents and larger-size homes. They would also permanently transform a thriving natural ecosystem and create ongoing maintenance requirements that would challenge residents long into the future.

CHANGED FOREVER

In evaluating the application for the development, the county required some entity to be responsible to manage and maintain the proposed new common areas and assets. The Lagoon Point Improvement Club, formed in 1960 to govern a clubhouse and social club, agreed to serve in this capacity. The county granted the permit, and the developer went forward with dredging and the massive construction project. The club, renamed the Lagoon Point Community Association in 2006, has continued to fulfill the maintenance and management role to this day with a board of directors and various committees.

Longtime residents recall their shock and dismay as the dredging began. Sisters Loretta Wilson and Ruth Stibre still live in the little fishing cabin their parents bought in 1956. They remember their father, an avid fisherman who had grown up on the St. Lawrence River, saying, "If they start dredging, they will have to keep dredging." He knew that the natural movement of the water would bring material back into the channels. He was shocked and angered that a real estate developer would be permitted to "rip up" terrain in this way. To this day, Stibre regrets the loss of the bird habitat that used to nurture 220 species of birds on their annual migrations. Yet both sisters acknowledge there were no active protests as the dredging and construction went forward. "Environmentalists didn't exist then like they do now," they say.

Aerial view of Lagoon Point. *Courtesy of Washington State Department of Ecology.*

Ferguson says, "Even then I knew they were ruining the land—it was being changed forever. We didn't want a mega-housing development, but that's what we got." People talked among themselves, recognizing their way of life was being changed forever, along with the land, but they did not see a way to stop the dredging. And so it went ahead.

TODAY

In addition to more than four hundred home sites, canals, private docks and boat moorages, Lagoon Point now has two boat ramps, a floating dock and launch area, a day-use parking lot for boat trailers for residents who do not have backyard moorage, a bulkhead, a jetty, common beach areas and a twenty-foot-long bridge that is locally famous for being the only bridge set entirely on Whidbey Island. (Five-hundred original lots were reduced in number over time as people have combined small lots or the odd triangular section that couldn't be built on.) The lagoon and the saltwater marsh are gone. Property values are robust.

When all this got underway in 1969, development occurred quickly and without organized protest. Today, in a political climate that is more environmentally conscious, strict shoreline management requirements and environmental protection laws would prohibit this scope of change in topography and habitat. With new critical-area protection standards, shoreline and critical-area regulations establish setbacks and buffers for new development. But since most lots in Lagoon Point are already developed and have been extensively modified, these regulations have a very limited impact.

Now, as wave and tidal action brings sand into the artificial waterways of Lagoon Point, periodic dredging must be performed to maintain navigability. It's a complicated process. Federal, state and county permits are required, and the approval process is arduous. The most recent dredging was completed in 2013, and the permitting process to allow it began in 2005.

The Lagoon Point newsletter from November 2013 describes the process: "Many requirements and options were involved and had to be coordinated with Island County Planning, Washington State Department of Fisheries and Wildlife, Department of Ecology, Department of Natural Resources and the Army Corps of Engineers. Contractors and consultants were also required for preparation of the permit and execution of the project." Dredging expenses were close to $625,000, paid for by assessments from Lagoon Point residents.

MITIGATION

One of Island County's requirements for dredging permission was that eelgrass be protected. Eelgrass is critical to fish habitat and a healthy marine ecosystem. Divers had to survey the eelgrass and move some of it to areas in the waterway that were suitable for it to grow. The area to be dredged had grown this eelgrass only in the previous two years as it had been too deep before the build-up of tide-related material. Ultimately, the divers did not return the transplanted grass to its original locations because it would not thrive in the newly dredged area—it would be healthier in its new location. The Lagoon Point Community Association must conduct ongoing monitoring of the eelgrass for the next five years to ensure its stability and vitality. In addition, people who replace, repair or construct private docks and gangways must incorporate an open grating system so eelgrass can receive light and remain healthy underneath the structures.

The community association's Environmental and Public Improvement Committee monitors water quality and makes sure that boats are maintained so they don't contribute to pollution. It examines water samples for independent assessment of water quality so that problems are caught early and addressed. Some homeowners farm oysters from their docks, and they need particularly clean water for this purpose.

CONTROVERSIES

Lagoon Point simmers with two ongoing controversies. One is long-standing, the other more recent.

Since the area was platted in 1950, beach access for fishing has been a source of conflict. When the population was smaller and residential development less intense, the situation was tolerable and manageable. But as the area was developed and the population of homeowners and of nonresident fishers grew, things got tense.

Because of historic peculiarities in property descriptions, some people own their tidelands—meaning that they can legally control access— and some do not. A few fishing areas are held in common by Lagoon Point residents, but many are not. Island County put in some SaniCans and roads for limited public access, but people disagree about what is county and what is private property. People often try to access public areas by deliberately or inadvertently trespassing on someone's property. The situation is fraught with conflict. Opinions are strong and passions run high.

Over time, property owners became increasingly disgruntled and then infuriated as growing numbers of fishers trespassed on their property— drinking, making noise, leaving trash and human waste, even using their decks and outdoor furniture. By the 1990s, some people began hiring off-duty sheriff's deputies to manage the problem during fishing season, particularly the steelhead season. Defense of privacy and property rights has extended to confronting hikers. Now some homeowners insist that nobody can even walk on their beaches. Many are wary and angry, and they sometimes openly confront each other and people from outside the community who ignorantly or actively disregard the rules.

In recent years, new permanent signs have been posted on road ends where there is public access, replacing sticks and strings that were often torn out by wind, waves and people. The boundaries and rules are becoming clearer.

A more recent conflict involves homeowners' assessments for dredging the waterways. Two lawsuits challenged the assessments by residents who do not have boat moorage because their home sites are located on the bluff or otherwise away from the water. Both lawsuits have resulted in findings, upheld on appeal, that assessments are mandatory for all Lagoon Point homeowners because the community (including the bluff) is a single plat with common areas that all must maintain. The assessments were not equal; people living on the canals ultimately paid for 70 percent of the project. Even though the latest dredging has been completed and assessments levied, there are still angry signs in the yards of residents on the bluff that urge people to VOTE NO ON DREDGING and STOP THE DREDGING SCAM.

NEXT

As a microcosm of a few hundred acres on a small island over a short period of time, Lagoon Point illustrates significant themes in how people and land interact. "Empty" land was sold, held, considered for military purposes and sold again. The owner and real estate developer accurately assessed the profitability of providing moorage and easy access for boats to the open water. At the time, environmental consciousness was not strong enough to mitigate the energy and profit-driven vision of the marketplace. When the economy and its emphasis on growth and development were the prime drivers of decision making about environmental resources, a thriving saltwater marsh was lost.

But nature cannot be completely subdued. The tides inexorably restore sand to the waterways, creating a new balance, requiring ongoing and expensive human intervention to maintain the market values of property and navigable waterways. Residents must resolve complicated issues of who owns what, who is responsible for what, who can make decisions, and what community standards will guide their interaction and future together.

Environmental concerns are now much more prevalent than in the late 1960s. People understand sustainability, appreciate the fragility and beauty of nature and value stewardship of earth's resources. They believe in the concept that "once it's gone, it's gone" and regret decisions made earlier in ignorance. At Lagoon Point, plans to mitigate earlier damage and to do no further harm to the environment are in place, and these goals are taken seriously.

Lagoon Point also illustrates that, when it comes to environmental damage, some problems can be fixed, but some cannot. The question is how to go forward wisely, preserving what we can, repairing what we can and balancing our desire for a healthy environment with our needs for shelter, sustenance and community.

And we hope for help from nature. Nature responds. Nature punishes and rebalances. Nature can heal and restore.

10

South Whidbey State Park

In 1977, loggers prepared to cut the last old-growth forest on South Whidbey Island. Islanders stood in front of the trees, starting a fifteen-year process that eventually saved the forest, preserving it as part of South Whidbey State Park. The experience informed a new generation of activists. Twenty years later, they stepped up to insist growth be managed to preserve the qualities of rural life on Whidbey Island.

THE PRESERVATION OF THE last old-growth forest, a dramatic fifteen-year battle that began in 1977, played out in packed courtrooms and newspapers across Washington State. The forest is now preserved as part of South Whidbey State Park.

This struggle set the stage for other Whidbey Island citizen actions in the years to come. In saving the trees, people learned how to mobilize and organize to fight for the health and beauty of their land.

Twenty years later, acting on their vibrant legacy and building on hard-won knowledge, another group of islanders organized. They demanded Island County adequately anticipate, manage and control development to ensure the rural character of the community was preserved and the environment protected. They insisted that county officials comply with Washington State's 1990 Growth Management Act (GMA) by writing a thoughtful and detailed plan to manage inevitable growth. The law recognized something many Whidbey Islanders intimately knew: unplanned and piecemeal growth threatened not only their environment but also their quality of life. They acted on the legacy from neighbors

Some of the trees in the park are over five hundred years old and still growing. *Courtesy of Whidbey Camano Land Trust.*

who stood in front of bulldozers two decades earlier. And some of them were the same people.

The history of activism, particularly in forcing elected officials and bureaucracies to abide by the law, resonates today in ongoing efforts to correct harmful or illegal practices and mitigate environmental damage. Today, some people are working to restore traditional public beach access. Others are working to protect salmon and shorelines. All use techniques of community organizing, public education and court action to move their work forward, learning from the past to achieve a preferred future.

PRECIOUS RESOURCE

South Whidbey State Park, with 4,500 feet of saltwater shoreline on Admiralty Inlet and a stand of magnificent old-growth forest, is a 347-acre treasure for camping, crabbing, clamming and hiking. The Wilbert Trail, named in honor of Harry and Myrl Wilbert, meanders through the forest. Harry Wilbert was an engineer who had helped reconstruct Pearl Harbor after the 1941 attack. Using his analytical skills and knowledge of science, he documented key factors in the legal case to save forest. He showed that if proposed logging went forward, the combination of steep slopes and inevitable soil erosion would threaten the existing state park that bordered on the forest.

The park's first eighty-five acres were leased by Washington State Parks in 1963 from the Washington State Department of Natural Resources (DNR). Additional acreage was added in 1970, when the shoreline portion was purchased by the parks agency. South Whidbey State Park was officially named in 1974.

The battle over the forest effectively began three years later, when Neil Colburn and Jack Noel went to a stand of trees to assess the job of cutting them down. They ran a small logging company called Shelterwood, featuring a little portable sawmill that they moved around Whidbey Island to selectively cut and mill trees on site. Colburn remembers the slogan: "We take your trees and turn them into your house."

Shelterwood was on a state contractor list, so the men had been notified of a bid by the DNR to clear-cut a forest parcel known as the "Classic U," which was adjacent to the South Whidbey State Park. It was one of a small portion of Washington lands set aside early in the state's history for eventual timber income to support the construction of public school buildings.

When Washington became a state in 1889, the federal government gave sections in every township for public building construction, including schools and universities. Initially managed by the State Land Commission, these properties became the responsibility of DNR when the department was established in 1957.

The clear-cut logging of the Classic U was intended to support new construction at the University of Washington. The area had been partially logged around 1900, but many huge trees that were hundreds of years old had been left standing. (The oldest tree there is believed to be more than five hundred years old.) It is possible that, with so many more easily handled smaller trees available for logging, these giants were spared as too difficult to harvest and transport. Whatever the reason, many old trees had survived in what is technically known as a lowland mature forest with some old-growth remnants. This is a very rare phenomenon in the Puget Sound lowlands.

TREE HUGGERS

What caught the attention of Colburn and Noel in the DNR's plan to clear-cut the area was the amount of wood DNR proposed to harvest; it was almost double the annual timber harvest for the entire island. So they went to see for themselves.

Colburn had recently moved to Whidbey from Berkeley, California, where he had helped establish the West Coast chapter of Viet Nam Veterans Against the War. Living in communes around the country, he had spent time doing low-impact horse logging in Vermont and learning about old-growth trees on the Russian River in California. He remembered thinking, "Wait a minute! Isn't this the last stand of old-growth forest on the island? I had started to think about having kids then, and I wanted them to be able to see what an old-growth tree looked like."

As the state bid moved through its bureaucratic process, the two men told friends about the threat to the forest. People started meeting at the Dog House Tavern in Langley to discuss the problem and mobilize to stop the DNR. They wore T-shirts that said, "Save the Trees." In June 1977, Noel stepped forward to file a lawsuit against the state DNR to challenge the cutting of the forest.

Not everyone on the island supported these newcomers, who were children of the counterculture with long hair and utopian visions. Some old-timers were outraged that these Johnny-come-lately outlanders, many from the alien state of California, would come to their turf, their island, and challenge their way of doing things. The newcomers were often marginalized and mocked as "tree huggers" and "long hairs" and viewed with hostile curiosity. The old-timers had no idea these strangers would change the fabric of their community in ways that would carry into the next century. And some old-timers could not have known they would soon be moved to stand with the hippies to save the forest for generations to come.

The DNR initially engaged in dialogue with the activists, but the agency soon declared the conversation over. It selected a logging company from Bellingham, Alpine Excavating Inc., for the $1.58 million state contract. The company prepared to begin the job by building roads through the forest to move equipment in and timber out.

Debora Valis remembers her friend Neil Colburn banging on her door. "Come quickly," he said. "Loggers are in the woods. It's an emergency!" She and her husband, Steve Shapiro, ran to the nearby forest, where logging trucks, bulldozers, and men with buzzing chainsaws were ready to start building roads for the clear-cut. "We stood in front of the trees. Some of us stood where a tree would fall if were to be cut down. We lay down in front of the bulldozers. We stared the loggers down. It was tense and terrifying, but they blinked first and left after a few hours' stand-off. We had no idea what we were doing. We just knew it was so obviously important," she recalled.

Steve Shapiro said, "We didn't want to have to do this. I had just hung out my shingle as an MD in Langley, and we didn't want to have to deal with controversy in the community. But we didn't feel we had a choice. We'd come from California, and we knew what could happen if we didn't act. We moved here to be in nature. We did that with intent. The trees were why we were here."

Litigation and Dialogue

In the tense aftermath of the confrontation in the forest, these and other activists formally incorporated as a nonprofit organization, Save the Trees. Articles of incorporation list seventeen people who sought legal standing to participate in litigation. The group connected with Seattle attorney Charles Ehlert, who was representing Jack Noel in his lawsuit against the DNR. When Save the Trees could legally join the lawsuit, Ehlert became the group's advocate as well. He deferred his fees, ultimately waiting twelve years for his last payment, which was delivered in a joyful community ceremony in September 1989.

A temporary injunction was granted, stopping the logging until the key lawsuit could be heard. Shapiro remembered, "It started with civil disobedience. The injunction was just the beginning. Then we had to win the case."

The lawsuit *Noel v. Cole* sought to stop the clear-cutting because the state had not abided by its 1971 legislation, the Washington State Environmental Policy Act (SEPA), which required an environmental impact statement (EIS) for projects in areas involving sensitive lands or endangered species. Harry Wilbert provided documentation on the likely impact of the proposed clear-cut, doing his own EIS on behalf of Save the Trees.

In an odd turn of events, two assistant state attorneys general faced off in a hearing. Assistant Attorney General Maryanne McGettigan argued for the state, holding that all state agencies had to comply with requirements for environmental impact statements that were in place as part of the Washington SEPA. Assistant Attorney General Ted Torve represented the DNR, arguing that the agency had the right to harvest Classic U for funds to build new buildings at the UW.

Thus began a process of dialogue, negotiation, litigation, legislative action and problem solving that lasted for the next fifteen years. In packed courtrooms and in newspapers throughout Washington State, new legal ground was promulgated. The DNR's logging practices changed to comply with SEPA.

In a historic agreement reached in 1981, a ten-year moratorium prohibited the cutting of the old-growth forest while the parties worked on options.

In April 1985, Governor Booth Gardner signed a bill adding the Classic U's old-growth trees to the state parks system. In 1992, the state parks agency traded an equivalent parcel of eastern Washington land to the DNR for logging in exchange for the unique tract on Whidbey Island. In 1992, Washington State Parks officially purchased 255 acres of rare old-growth forest through a trust land agreement with the DNR. At this point, the Classic U was officially added to the South Whidbey State Park.

The final addition to the park, the "Ryan addition" of 7.3 acres, was added in 2006. The community came together to raise $383,000 to purchase this small triangle-shaped piece of land so important to the park's integrity and beauty.

Today, Friends of South Whidbey State Park help care for the park, repairing trails, removing invasive plants, leading walks and keeping a close eye on this precious resource.

POWER TO THE PEOPLE

The fight by the people who rallied to form Save the Trees reveals how people are moved to action. The process begins with impulsive, even desperate resistance. More experienced activists are joined by others who are moved by the threat to something they believe is precious. Determined people then master the complexities of the bureaucratic and political systems, exercise political power, educate their communities, engage the courts, forge alliances and find creative solutions.

The Save the Trees battle offers insight into the many ways people define effective advocacy and the range of compromise and dialogue they are willing to accept. It brings into high relief the competing strategies and internecine battles of various sectors of the environmental movement. But most of all, it provides yet another example of how the unique natural resources of Whidbey Island have called so many people to their service in ways they never expected. As Joseph Campbell stated, "We must be willing to let go of the life we planned so as to accept the life that is waiting for us."

A peaceful place to sit in the old-growth forest of South Whidbey State Park. *Courtesy of the Whidbey Camano Land Trust.*

The Save the Trees saga of smart, passionate community organizing combined with astute political and legal strategies set an example for another group of Whidbey Island activists two decades later. They, too, employed the tried-and-true principles of grass-roots organizing, including community mobilization, educating and lobbying public officials, finding compromises to move forward and refusing to give up.

CITIZEN ACTIVISM AND GROWTH

A sweeping new issue erupted in the early 1990s when Island County elected officials refused to comply with a state-mandated requirement to plan and manage sustainable growth especially in rural areas, and a new group of activists convened to address it. In response, members of eight organizations concerned with the environment and advocating for careful development joined together in 1997, forming the Citizens Growth Management Coalition.

The state had adopted the Growth Management Act in 1990, asserting that uncoordinated, uncontrolled and unplanned development presents a danger to the environment, the economy, and citizens' quality of life. The GMA was designed to rely on the strong tradition of local control rooted in the political and geographic diversity of the state's communities. In essence, the GMA mandated local governments to manage growth by identifying and protecting critical areas, designating areas for intensive development based on the availability of infrastructure and spelling-out detailed regulations governing future development. All of this was to be expressed in comprehensive plans prepared by local governments. A Growth Management Hearings Board was established to monitor and enforce local compliance in the preparation of these plans.

For seven years, Island County's three elected commissioners failed to comply with the GMA. Finally in 1997, faced with the threat of major economic sanctions from the state, the commissioners began a process to prepare a plan. Many observers thought the planning process was not being taken seriously and that county officials would do the least they could to forestall state sanctions while waiting for the political winds to shift away from GMA principles.

Precedents existed for citizen activism in growth issues. Throughout the 1980s, other citizen-based efforts on the island worked successfully to implement sensible development that would protect sensitive areas and mitigate sprawl.

The Whidbey Environmental Action Network began in 1985 to stop roadside herbicide spraying. The organization was among the first to recognize that the county was going to resist the GMA. It began working to ensure a GMA-compliant plan would be produced.

FARSIGHTED PLANNING

Citizens for Sensible Development formed in the '80s on Whidbey Island to lobby for well-conceived regulations to control growth for this beloved rural community situated in its precious and fragile natural environment. The group's first battle was over the expansion of a small local airport. Objections centered on noise and the aesthetic challenges to the rural character of the community. These arguments were not persuasive for eager officials who had obtained grants for the construction and were ready to move forward on airport expansion. So the activists took a different tack: they conducted economic and fiscal analysis that showed the proposed airport would lose money and would be an ongoing drain on public resources. In 1990, after a two-year fight, the airport expansion idea was shelved.

By 1997, everyone knew growth on the island was inevitable. WEAN, Citizens for Sensible Development and six other groups who had formed the Citizens Growth Management Coalition that year wanted growth to be thoughtfully controlled, with regulations that were sensible and well conceived. They wanted a GMA-compliant, comprehensive plan that was legal, fair and farsighted. So they wrote it themselves.

John Graham, who chaired this group, remembers that the coalition produced a 120-page plan as an alternative to the superficial and incomplete growth plan being proposed by Island County. When the plan was presented, many more citizens were inspired to join. The political power shift became more evident to elected officials. They were not used to this kind of interaction and scrutiny. For the next three years, the coalition kept the pressure up. "It was the beginning of the end for the so-called good-old-boy network that had run the county for decades," Graham recalled.

Coalition members engaged in ongoing planning and research. They put together detailed proposals on twenty-seven issues related to growth—everything from preserving small farms to rules for storm water drainage to low-income housing. They presented their ideas in public testimony, op-ed pieces, letters to newspaper editors and community forums. They negotiated with county planners, seeking solutions and compromises to help the county prepare a comprehensive and meaningful GMA plan that was responsive to local concerns and respectful of different perspectives. They worked with other groups, farmers and property rights advocates, seeking productive dialogue and creative solutions each side could support. Many old foes began to move from an adversarial stance to creative problem solving. The position, "Don't fight each other, fight the problem" produced solid results.

SHIFT IN POWER

Jim Larsen, a longtime Whidbey Island newspaperman, commented, "The fewer the people, the fewer the land use rules." In a sparsely populated area, such as Whidbey Island used to be, development was also sparse, diffuse and often invisible. As the population grew, people sought more rules to "stop my neighbor from doing what I don't want him to do," as Larsen succinctly puts it. By the time of the GMA, ordinary citizens had become concerned with rules that could both control their own actions and empower them to stop others.

The coalition educated the community on these complex and often technical issues. It recognized that, if people understood good growth management was to their long-term advantage, they would be less likely to reverse the forward momentum in future elections or lawsuits. Graham said, "If you are dealing with something complex like the character of a rural place, it can't depend on having the right people in office because that can change. And it can't depend on just on winning court battles, because those decisions can be overturned. What works is convincing enough citizens of the validity of your case so that the whole political center of gravity begins to shift."

Coalition members organized to elect candidates to shift political power away from laissez-faire officials, replacing them at the ballot box with others who understood and supported long-range and comprehensive regulation of growth. When necessary, they took legal action, taking issues to the Growth Management Hearings Board when they could not make satisfactory progress with local testimony and negotiation. In June 1999, the board decided three-quarters of the growth issues that came before it in the coalition's favor, requiring the county to revise its growth plan to reflect these rulings. The coalition then monitored the progress of the plan revision to ensure nothing slipped through the cracks. In 2001, the county submitted a GMA-compliant Comprehensive Plan to guide and manage growth into the future.

Emerging Stewardship

In our individual journeys, we find others who share our visions of how the world should be. Together we learn to shape our future. That's what happened when the last of the old-growth forest on Whidbey Island was threatened. It caught the attention of a group of concerned people and set in motion a sustained community effort to change environmental policy. Lessons were learned that informed community organizing to address other environmental threats. These diverse grass-roots efforts helped build community consciousness, engage creativity and grit, clarify values and move politics to a new normal. Ordinary people did what common wisdom said was impossible.

As Malcolm Gladwell writes in *David and Goliath: Underdogs, Misfits, and the Art of Battling Giants*, "What we consider valuable in our world arises out of these kinds of lopsided conflicts, because the act of facing overwhelming odds produces greatness and beauty."

11

Double Bluff Beach

*P*ublic beach access is a complex issue as shorelines become more populated. Double Bluff Beach is a story about beach access—with a happy ending. People came together, with different political and personal views, because they agreed that this iconic and wildly beautiful place belonged to everyone. Government officials found creative ways to make sure the beach and tidelands remain available to the public. But in other parts of the island, beach access is still a knotty problem.

SOME SAY DOUBLE BLUFF State and County Park is South Whidbey Island's best-kept secret. Local people have known about it for a long time. Islanders enjoyed the beach and tidelands well before it was a designated park. As word of beautiful Double Bluff got out, mainlanders began to find their way to this magical place. They come by ferry for a day or the weekend to walk the beach, dig for clams, wade in shallow tidelands, fly kites and toss sticks into the surf for dogs to fetch.

It wasn't always easy. In the old days, a pile of boulders placed at the bottom of the county parking lot at the end of Double Bluff Road blocked what was, at the time, the only public access. Intrepid beach goers, however, weren't about to let a few boulders get in their way. They simply trespassed across nearby private lands. People put up more barriers, but visitors just kept coming until the situation came to a head.

PARK FOR THE PEOPLE

Double Bluff Beach follows a wild and beautiful coastline about four miles along Useless Bay, the same bay into which Maxwelton Creek drains. (See Chapter 3.) At the southern tip, it becomes the dramatic Double Bluff Point, which is often depicted on tourist brochures or used to illustrate stories about Whidbey Island. Then the beach turns east along Mutiny Bay, and the bluff recedes. Driftwood forts and sculptures dot the long stretch of sand along with boulders of all sizes.

Double Bluff is a beach for all seasons. In summer, the more adventuresome skim board along thin waves that rhythmically wash up and slide back from the sandy shore. When it's cold and blustery, the kite sailors show up in wetsuits looking for wind to power their boards across the water. Each year, as many as 150 islanders start off the New Year with a bone-chilling splash during the annual Double Bluff Polar Bear Dive.

The defining feature of the park is the large bluff. About a quarter mile south of the park entrance, the bluff reaches about one hundred feet, its greatest height. This bluff, along with a similar one on the north side of

Intrepid Polar Bear divers at Double Bluff Beach on New Year's Day 2014. *Courtesy of the South Whidbey Record.*

Opposite, bottom: Aerial view of Double Bluff, 2006. The image shows feeder bluffs, second-growth forests, freshwater wetlands, streams and a small lake. *Courtesy of Washington State Department of Ecology.*

Iconic Double Bluff as seen from across Deer Lake, located to the east. *Courtesy of Whidbey Camano Land Trust.*

the bay, was created by an immense slide of glacial clay. The two bluffs are the oldest formations known on the island, visible evidence of the repeated advance and receding of glaciers.

The land on top of the bluff extends away from the beach and into an area with feeder bluffs, second-growth forests, freshwater wetlands, streams and a small lake. Many species of wildlife are found here, including bald eagles, great blue herons, peregrine falcons, gulls and pileated woodpeckers.

The Whidbey Camano Land Trust assisted Island County in the purchase of a twenty-acre portion of the upper bluff area, the Wahl Road Forest. It is part of a larger track, including Double Bluff Beach, which the land trust has declared a priority area.

The bluff is a mixture of gravel, sand, clay and topsoil. At this favored spot for climbing, people of all ages scramble up the steep slopes. They slip and slide in the loose sand and soil, looking for a branch to grab. There isn't much vegetation to be found because of the constantly shifting sands and subsequent erosion. Erosion has caused the bluff to recede as much as one hundred feet in the past forty years. Just like the climbers, trees and other plants have trouble getting a foothold.

STUNNING VIEWS AND PLAY

Most of what the state owns is tidelands. The sandy, shallow slope of Useless Bay creates mudflats that can vary in size by more than 2,500 feet from high to low tide. At high tide, there is only a thin strip of rocky beach that follows the bluff from its southern end at Double Bluff Point until it reaches the north end and the entrance to what is now the county park. There the beach becomes an upland, a large triangle-shaped piece of ground covered with vegetation and driftwood. The upland is tucked into the bluff as it curves and drops off toward Double Bluff Road.

"Go at ebb tide, when the tide's going out," the experienced beachcombers will tell you. "That's when the beach is nearly twice its normal size and you see more. But keep an eye on the tide." The tide flats are what caused Charles Wilkes to name the bay "Useless" in 1841. Captain George Vancouver is said to have gotten stuck there in 1792.

Despite the name, visitors find many uses for the bay. Children romp and play in the shallow water while others dig for geoduck or butter clams. Beach walkers search for colorful stones or poke at barnacle-covered rocks. Some

View of the uplands, 2006. The uplands were once privately owned and, in the 1950s, were the site of a fishing resort. Small private cabins remain at the toe of the bluff, where it meets the uplands. *Courtesy of Washington State Department of Ecology.*

Sunbathers enjoy the expanse of tidelands at low tide. *Private collection.*

Double Bluff Point. Directly in front is the beach along Useless Bay; as the beach rounds the corner to the east, the water flows into Mutiny Bay. *Courtesy of Washington State Department of Ecology.*

may find a chunk of black, flakey peat. Occasionally, a sharp-eyed forager comes across fossilized mammoth bones.

Views are stunning from just about everywhere. Start from the visitor entrance at the north end. Walk south across the upland and along the beach and tide flats. Gaze east, out over the water, and the Cascade Mountains tower in front of you. Continue to stroll southward and the high-rises of Seattle are soon visible above the skyline, dwarfed by the snow-capped peak of Mount Rainier, nearly one hundred miles away.

The beach turns east at Double Bluff Point. Walk around the Chuckanut Formation, a ten-foot-high sandstone boulder, near the Point. The Vashon glacier transported the boulder from the Chuckanut Mountains more than forty miles away. Keep walking around the point along Mutiny Bay and the Olympic Mountain Range comes into view.

RESORTS AND TRESPASSERS

The beach uplands have been privately held since 1875. Eventually, they became six shoreline lots. Each includes part of the sandy beach and a portion of the steep bluff behind them. People trespassed across these lots for many years, primarily the three lots closest to the parking lot, on their way to the state-owned beach and tidelands.

In the 1930s and '40s, three small cabins were built at the south end of the uplands. They are nestled against the toe, where the steep bluff rises above the flat beach area. There was no direct access from Double Bluff Road, so the owners built a cedar walkway that goes from the parking lot along the toe of the bluff and across the three empty lots nearest the road—property that would later become a fishing resort.

The tidal eddies of Useless Bay are home to small herring and candlefish that attract game fish of all kinds. Similar bays and points on the beaches of Whidbey make the island a popular sport fishing destination and, in earlier years, the home of several fishing resorts.

"Good spinning and fly fishing at Double Bluff Resort," read brochures in the '50s. Double Bluff Resort sat on the lots adjacent to the parking lot. The resort featured eight two-bedroom cabins, built on fill that had been placed on the bluff side of a 187-foot log-pile bulkhead. Nearby storage held forty boats. A café offered breakfast. Lots of people came, including well-known Seattleites such as the players from the Seattle Rainiers, the city's minor-league baseball team. Visitors who didn't want to drive to the resort could fly in by seaplane.

The tide flats of Useless Bay could be a challenge to the owner of the resort, Chris Jensen. William Haroldson, in his book *Resorts of South Whidbey Island*, describes how Jensen dealt with the problem. Using a surplus World War II weapons carrier with a forklift attached to the front, he picked up the fishing boat with the forklift and then boarded the eager fishermen onto the weapons carrier. Skillfully avoiding the sinkholes in the tidal muck, he transported the entire rig across the tide flats to deeper water.

In 1955, the resort became Johnston's Double Bluff Resort when it was sold to Esther and Crawford Johnson. The couple remodeled the café and served both breakfast and dinner. "Sitting on the fly fishing bay of Whidbey Island," is the way they advertised the resort in newspapers as far away as Spokane.

By 1960, the fishing resort was no longer in business, and the Newlin family purchased the property. A fire that swept through the resort in 1965 destroyed most of the cabins. Those that survived were sold and moved, and the property was cleared.

Double Bluff beach is an accreting beach, a situation where shifting sand and other deposits delivered by swirling tides increase its size. By 1960, the upland beach had grown. The high tide mark moved about 250 feet away from the three original cabins, leaving their boat ramps sitting in beach vegetation. Tidal waters had taken their toll on the log-pile bulkhead in front of the old resort, too. It was in a sad state of neglect, the fill behind it washed away, replaced by about twenty-eight feet of upland beach vegetation.

Alice Newlin, daughter of the original Newlin purchasers, inherited the property in 1991 along with her daughter, Jill Newlin Reed. The trickle of trespassers had, by this time, become a steady stream of beachcombers, clam diggers, horseback riders, motorcyclists, three wheelers, windsurfers, kayakers and children on school fieldtrips.

Although there were no structures on the Newlin/Reed property except for the old wooden bulkhead, a concerned Jill Reed and her husband, Bruce, erected a six-foot-high opaque wooden fence with a large No Trespassing sign. It ran one hundred feet from the toe of the bluff, along the side of the parking lot, until it reached the high water mark on the beach. That didn't slow people down. They just made their way around the fence and across the Newlin/Reed property.

IRREPLACEABLE TREASURE

Bringing matters to a head in 1988, the Reeds, along with Alice Newlin, decided to build a vacation home on their property. They filed a petition to build a concrete bulkhead as a replacement for the old log-pile bulkhead and proposed to place 240 cubic yards of fill behind it. Because they proposed to replace the old bulkhead, the Reed-Newlins hoped to "grandfather" their application, avoiding the more complex requirements contained in Washington State's 1971 Shoreline Management Act (SMA).

Initially, the Island County hearing examiner denied the Reed-Newlin application. But the Island County Board of Commissioners overturned the decision and approved it. Then things got even more complicated.

The state Department of Ecology disapproved a portion of the application. It ruled that the proposed 240 yards of fill were "inconsistent with the Island County Shoreline Master Program prohibition of fill on tidelands" and said that the old log-pile bulkhead was in such poor repair that the proposed concrete bulkhead could not be considered an upgrade. It was new construction and would have to meet the requirements of the SMA. But the state Shoreline Hearings Board overruled Ecology to allow construction of the bulkhead as originally proposed.

The Reeds and Alice Newlin also filed a damage lawsuit that was heard in Snohomish County. The judge ruled against them but instructed Larry Kwarsick, representing Island County as director of planning, "to work things out."

Kwarsick set out to find a solution. He knew how special Double Bluff was to the people of Whidbey Island and to many mainlanders. He began to think about how to preserve it as a park. Initially, he approached the Reeds and Newlin with a purchase offer of $600,000. He secured $63,400 from state resources and then contacted Mike Shelton, one of three members of the Island County Board of Commissioners, for help in putting together the balance.

Shelton initially balked at the idea of purchasing the Double Bluff lots. The three lots were valued at $1.4 million. He was concerned that the county was being asked to ignore the private property rights of the owners by offering substantially less than the market value. He felt that the county was trying to "regulate the value out of the property."

At hearings on the matter, Shelton was impressed by the cross-section of conservationists and developers, usually in opposition to one another, who collectively spoke in favor of this purchase. One longtime resident, known to be very conservative, told him, "If this land is developed, we won't ever find another piece like it. It's a treasure we can never replace." Shelton, steadfast in his commitment to his constituents, listened closely.

Kwarsick seized on an opportunity created by Washington State's 1990 Growth Management Act. Included in the legislation was an option for counties to impose and collect an additional excise tax on the sale of real property. The money could then be used to apply for matching state funds. The funds were combined to form a county-based Conservation Futures Fund to be available to acquire and maintain designated conservation areas such as Double Bluff Beach. With the support and hard work of Shelton and Kwarsick, county commissioners approved the creation of the fund.

Next, Shelton and Kwarsick turned to the Trust for Public Lands, a national nonprofit organization that conserves land for public space. They asked Phil Pearl, the local director, to assist in what became a successful negotiation for purchase of the three Double Bluff beach lots at the market price.

Island County commissioners approved the purchase in November 1993. Commissioner Mac McDowell, commenting on the high purchase price, noted that "access to water in Island County is at some speed disappearing." He concluded that the money was well spent for the valuable public access to Double Bluff. Shelton noted that the purchase would "greatly enhance the ability to avoid infringement on private property owners in the area."

Shelton recalled, "During my fifteen years as a commissioner, the Double Bluff purchase is one of the things I am most proud of." Kwarsick feels the same way: "The creation of the Conservation Futures Fund happened because of Double Bluff and then led to many more valuable acquisitions."

PARK STATUS AND BEACH ACCESS CONTROVERSY

The Double Bluff tidelands are now Double Bluff State Park. The upland property, purchased from the Reed-Newlins, provides access and is operated by Island County as Double Bluff County Park and Beach Access. A volunteer group, Friends of Double Bluff, helps to maintain the property. The county park contains bathrooms, outdoor showers, and picnic areas at the access point. There is also an off-leash dog park. The original cabins still stand to the south of the park, up against the bluff. One has become a comfortable bed and breakfast. The entire area continues to be enjoyed by many local and mainland visitors.

Although the Double Bluff story ends well, there are still many places where public access to beaches remains a problem. Beach front, as McDowell noted in 1993, is fast disappearing.

"Everyone deserves access to our beaches," said Judy Lynn, a member of the Whidbey Camano Land Trust. Judy donated 755 feet of private tidelands to make them accessible to all. Unfortunately not everyone feels that way. There are some who deliberately build barriers and block access because they live on a public beach but don't want to share it.

Mike McVay visited a public beach with his son one day, only to be yelled at by a nearby property owner. He created an organization called Whidbey Island Land and Shore Trust to "identify, map, sign, and preserve access to the public shorelines of Island County for the legal and rightful use of its citizens, for future generations." Now McVay spends his days poring through plats, zoning maps, tax reports and other dusty documents from several county departments, and sometimes state offices, to figure out if a property is publicly owned.

About one hundred public beach access points exist on Whidbey Island. Not all of them are known or used by the public. They are becoming more valuable, and the source of more controversy, as houses are built along the shore.

Although only a few high-profile beach ownership disputes have made local news, McVay believes the problem is serious. He is gradually persuading county officials that he is right, and they have hired a researcher to help identify and accurately catalogue points of public access. McVay's hope is that with his help, and additional effort on the part of the county, people will be able to simply walk to the island's beautiful beaches without fear of confrontation just as they are now able to do at Double Bluff Park.

12

Saratoga Woods Preserve

*O*ut a winding, rural road, a former family farm was to become a planned residential development of some 130 units. Neighbors began immediately to organize opposition to the mammoth project. Central to their effort was the challenge to require Island County to follow the state Growth Management Act and establish a comprehensive growth management plan. A six-year effort concluded with Island County complying with state law and a new vigilance among residents to hold the county's elected officials accountable to it. The 118-acre farm was purchased, protected and donated to Island County for a park.

DIANE KENDY SHARED HER scrapbook detailing the six-year process to save the woods on Saratoga. Her three-inch binder is filled with photocopies of newspaper articles, public notices, letters to the editor, flyers for fundraising events and more. The documents chronicle the perseverance of an extraordinary grass-roots effort. A small group of citizens knew something was inherently wrong about a proposed development outside the town of Langley. They did something about it.

"They were pretty ordinary things, just a lot of them," Kendy said of the activities leading to the victory. "We read public notices, went to public meetings...Lots of people wrote letters. Many raised money to pay legal fees because we knew we were in for court battles with Island County." The community "became involved and vocal to stop the bending or breaking of the laws. We all wanted to protect the quality of life we loved."

Out for a stroll in the Saratoga Woods. *Courtesy of Whidbey Camano Land Trust.*

For Kendy, the story began in 1995, soon after she moved to Whidbey Island from California with her husband, Michael Nutt, a retired violinist from the Los Angeles Philharmonic Orchestra. They "loved the forest, the quiet and the community."

Kendy noticed a "For Sale" sign on Saratoga Road. "Our property was next to the forest being sold," she explained. "We were stunned to realize that we could have a huge development right next door. But our real concern, after the land and nature itself, was that the developers really had no money. So we feared that they would scrape the land, run out of money and then leave. All of us would have to deal with the problems of the bare land. We were really motivated to stop what was clearly a bad plan."

They "kept the issue alive" for the next six years. "Besides letters and articles and fundraisers, there were formal complaints, lawsuits and more. Kendy and those working with her "realized we needed to be part of the process." Kendy's scrapbook reveals an extraordinary tale of how determined citizen action preserved a quality of life and the character of a community. From the fundraising came two community groups that still operate eighteen years later—the Saratoga Chamber Orchestra and the Whidbey Island Garden Tour. So that everyone could know about the effort, she donated the complete, original records to the South Whidbey Historical Society in Langley. The story illustrates how a sense of place develops and becomes a rallying cry for action to shape the future.

Before That Sign

In 1952, Sam and Katherine Wood purchased a 120-acre rural property about two and a half miles out Saratoga Road from Langley. The property had been newly logged except for a small fringe of forest near the house. It had been on the market for a while. Sam had dreamed of living on an island, owning waterfront land and having enough room both to provide for his family and to land the airplane he loved to fly. The property fit the criteria, and the Woods moved with their three children from near Marysville to rural Whidbey Island. Sixty-one years later, Katherine Wood recounted the life they created:

> Our house had wood heat only. We had cattle and pigs, gardens and fruit trees. Mostly, it was for our own use, but we did sell some milk and berries. We smoked ham and bacon, made cheese and lived pretty much on our land. I would make sandwiches, and we'd go for walks in the forest. It was all mosses and ferns. The boys and I would sit on a downed log and have our sandwich. I took all our guests for walks in the forest. It was beautiful, a real treasure.
>
> Sam commuted to his machine shop in Everett. For years, he took the ferry but when he got the landing strip on the top of our property, he could commute by plane. He did love flying. It was his hobby. And part of his business was building and selling planes.
>
> Years after the kids grew up and left, we were getting old and the property was too much. Taxes were getting to be bad, too. So we sold it to some people who presented a lovely plan with homes on five- or ten-acre lots. They were excited about the airstrip and planned to use it in the development. We moved to Orcas Island. A couple of years later, we heard that the first people had lost their funding and another group took over.

Save the Woods

When Kendy saw the sign in 1995, she began to research at the Island County office in Coupeville. She read the plan for a large residential development submitted by Resource Group Inc., Whidbey/KSC LLC. It looked like a subdivision complete with cul-de-sacs. Kendy also learned that the county had not even begun to write a comprehensive plan to manage growth as required by the 1990 GMA. The county was still using a decades-old zoning code with wide-open zoning that would probably invite destruction of the very beauty and rural environment she and her neighbors embraced. Kendy got busy, enlisting the help of neighbors to protect the environment in their neighborhood.

The campaign began when three women—Kendy, Fran Abel and Betty Azar—founded Save the Woods on Saratoga (SWS) to "protect the natural and human environment of South Whidbey Island, including its rural character, vulnerable groundwater, wildlife habitat, and valuable wetlands." They hired an attorney and developed a plan to educate people, raise funds, challenge attitudes in county government and protect the unique characteristics of one part of rural Whidbey Island.

Through the hard work of this long process, the group achieved some exciting successes. The first victory, according to Kendy, was turning the county board of commissioners against "vacating" (essentially giving) some county-owned view property rights across Saratoga Road to the developer group. Scores of citizens attended a public meeting to discuss the proposal, and the commissioners agreed to keep the property.

Help came from other groups. Whidbey Environmental Action Network (WEAN) began a series of appeals to the Western Washington Growth Management Hearings Board to force the issue of Island County's failure to follow state law.

The Washington legislature had passed the GMA to halt the uncoordinated and unplanned growth that threatened the environment, sustainable development and the overall quality of life in the state. Building on the tradition of local government control and regional diversity, the GMA required state and local governments to manage growth and discourage sprawl. Essential to the process was the law's requirement that each county develop and implement comprehensive plans for zoning and growth. The GMA gave counties more than three years to develop, approve and file a comprehensive plan. The deadline for Island County was December 1994.

By the summer of 1995, Island County had not even begun the process of creating the plan. WEAN filed a complaint with the hearings board, which invalidated much of Island County's existing zoning code because it contributed to sprawl. That decision marked the end of the planned development on Saratoga. A year later, when a destination resort was proposed for that property, WEAN filed yet another complaint to force the issue of a comprehensive plan to comply with the GMA. When Island County finally wrote a new plan, WEAN challenged it because it didn't comply with the law. Back-and-forth legal appeals ended up with the Washington State Court of Appeals, which upheld most of WEAN's case.

SWS financed these legal processes, and the group was often listed as "friends of the court." During this time, several local environmental groups formed the Growth Management Coalition to write the plan. The coalition negotiated and consulted with many groups of citizens and county government in a four-year process that paralleled the SWS effort. SWS continued its involvement by writing letters, participating in meetings and conducting research. Along with many other community groups, it held fundraising events that raised resources to cover the cost of legal bills and bring many others into the grass-roots movement. Fran Abel, one of the founders of SWS, ran for county commissioner, narrowly losing but raising the public profile on the topics of growth and quality of life.

But despite this activity, the county board of commissioners continued to delay writing the required new comprehensive plan, providing a loophole that the developer might exploit. SWS filed a lawsuit against Whidbey/KSC LLC in Skagit County Superior Court. It contended that the size of the planned destination resort-conference center was beyond the scope permitted by the GMA. The developer petitioned the court to let it proceed under the existing zoning codes. The judge ruled that the decision on that petition must be decided in trial. That ruling was projected to delay the final decision by months.

When Island County adopted a new comprehensive plan that did not include a master plan or destination resorts, the developer sued to have its permit application considered vested; this status would allow it to be processed. After months of debate, Island County withdrew the permit application at the request of its public works director.

BUY PROPERTY TO PROTECT IT

Island County's final comprehensive plan did not allow master plan resorts anywhere in the county. With that decision, SWS once again considered buying the property.

Kendy described the situation. "I think the owners were thoroughly disgusted with us. They wouldn't talk to us. Through Cary Peterson, then president of the Whidbey Camano Land Trust, we connected with a new board member, Phil Pearl, who was a land protection specialist with significant negotiation experience. He had the expertise. Phil met with the owners and negotiated a purchase price of $750,000. We became the fundraising arm of the land trust."

Tree stump still filled with life in the Saratoga Woods. *Courtesy of Whidbey Camano Land Trust and photographer Mark Sheehan.*

When prospective donors toured the forest, fundraising went quickly. They responded to the quiet, the ferns and mosses and the wildlife just as the Wood family had done. They wanted the property to remain a beautiful, natural area. Hundreds of people donated to save the place that so many considered magical. In just seven months, SWS had raised enough to buy the property. In October 2001, the land trust purchased the property and put a conservation easement on it. Then it donated the 118 acres to Island County for a public park.

Whew! Finally, hardworking SWS leaders could take a deep breath and rest. The forest was now the Saratoga Woods Preserve, public property and protected forever.

NEW TOOLS TO PROTECT THE LAND

While the local activists were working to save threatened woods on Saratoga Road, the directors of the Whidbey Camano Land Trust began to realize that the organization needed to change too. Kathleen Landel, then a board member, recalled how that shift began to happen. "In 2000, when Phil Pearl joined the board, he brought expertise and enthusiasm for the mission of protecting land by acquisition. At the same time, the trust's leadership saw that the community had the interest and the capacity to protect the natural areas people loved."

Landel explained:

> *Board members attended the national Land Trust Rally, a professional conference in Portland, during the final year of the Saratoga Woods effort. There we experienced a galvanizing sense of purpose and learned many new tools to do the important work of our mission. Successfully saving the Saratoga Woods and realizing more clearly how important our mission was challenged us to help guide the land trust to be all that it could be. That meant we needed to move from being all-volunteer and become a professional organization with land protection expertise. So, we did.*

In 2008, a small parcel was added to the protected land. Joani and Dale Boose donated a conservation easement on part of their beloved property, which adjoins the preserve. It is protected and not open to the public; the Booses wanted to ensure that, as many people enjoy the public preserve, wildlife would have a safe place there, too.

Different Sign on Saratoga Road

At the back of the small parking lot at the Saratoga Woods Preserve, you'll see a kiosk, the roofed information board common in parks and nature areas. Behind the locked glass door, a wooden panel shows an interesting collection of maps, notices of work parties and projects and some guidelines for visitor behavior. Unspoken but very present is the welcome to all who come to the Saratoga Woods Preserve.

This place, an Island County public area for walking and running, has become beloved to thousands of locals and visitors. Not only is it beautiful and interesting, but it also belongs to all of us. When people saw that it might be developed, their love for this place galvanized them to help control and shape the future of their neighborhood. Conversations during the campaign to Save the Woods on Saratoga reinforced the community imperative to protect land, including its quality of life and its precious, limited resources. People spoke about generations to come, about taking responsibility for our actions and about deciding for ourselves what kind of a place we want to make.

Protecting this beautiful forest also changed how many residents expressed their citizenship. They became more involved, held elected officials accountable and challenged Island County government to represent all its constituents, not just the favored groups. In short, people insisted that Island County follow state laws even when the county commissioners didn't like them.

This amazing place, the Saratoga Woods Preserve, comes from a remarkable story of love of the land and a community's determination to care for it—forever.

13

The Trillium
Community Forest

*B**y November 2009, the great recession had settled firmly in Island County. Developers*
defaulted on a $4.9 million loan to turn a large property north of Freeland into a
housing development for which they had preliminary approval from the county. A consortium
of banks wanted to sell their sinking asset quickly. Soon the Whidbey Camano Land Trust
began an intense fundraising campaign to purchase the property. Seven months and more
than 1,500 donors later, the land trust bought the property for wildlife habitat, watershed
protection and shared, low-impact community use. Now community groups are learning to
work together to restore and enjoy this forest.

FEBRUARY 10, 2010, DIDN'T seem like an auspicious day at first. The cool
weather with sunbreaks was pretty typical for winter around South Whidbey
Island. On the ferry from the mainland back to Whidbey Island, Pat Powell,
executive director of the Whidbey Camano Land Trust, and Tom Cahill,
then board president, chatted about their meeting with executives from
Shoreline Bank.

Cahill was newly installed as president and deeply committed to the
mission of local land protection. He and Powell had just signed, on behalf
of the full board, an option to purchase agreement on a square mile of
renewing forest. They had committed the land trust to raise more than $4
million in just four months. Looking at each other, they asked, "What have
we done?"

The four months would race by. Somehow, the land trust had to develop
an effective plan to raise lots of money—more money and more rapidly than

anyone involved had ever done. What was needed was a financial miracle. Those were in short supply during the great recession.

The prospect hadn't seemed so daunting when staff and board discussed it multiple times during the previous months. Immediately following a robust celebration in 2009 that honored the land trust's twenty-five years of local, grass-roots land protection, the topic of saving this property came up. Yes, it was the largest, privately owned forest remaining on Whidbey Island. Yes, it fed three important watersheds. Yes, it was near South Whidbey State Park, an important connector for people and wildlife.

But 2009–10 was a tough period to raise money, even for a project that clearly fit the land trust's mission. People were uncertain about the future and eager to conserve their personal assets. Powell, experienced and successful at securing grant funds for land protection, knew there would be no grant money for this project. If it were to happen, all the money would have to come from private donors. Conversations at the land trust concluded with "we have to try"—even though it seemed impossible.

Yet there was reason to believe that people would step up in this Herculean effort. Longtime residents had vigorously protested a brutal clear-cut two decades before and the proposed sprawl-style development that followed. Deep ire at local politicians who bent tax rules for developers and equally deep grief over the loss of important open space could mobilize residents to help save the property. Horseback riders who enjoyed trails on the old logging roads had stated their interest in helping to secure resources that would be needed.

Water. Wildlife. People. The whole community would benefit if the property could be saved. With the signed option to purchase agreement in hand, the race was on.

A Look Back

The square mile of what is now the Trillium Community Forest straddles a high ridge between Greenbank and Freeland. Thickly forested, the area was logged selectively between 1875 and 1975, following the historic patterns of timber harvests elsewhere on Whidbey Island. As Richard White explained in his book *Land Use, Environment, and Social Change: The Shaping of Island County*, settlers in the nineteenth and early twentieth century logged areas on Whidbey Island, paid the property tax and then learned that they had

What the Trillium Community Forest could have looked like—filled with houses and roads. *Courtesy of the Whidbey Camano Land Trust.*

no way to continue to pay the tax burden. Many abandoned their lands, and the title reverted to Island County by default. The county was happy to transfer these lands to owners who could pay some taxes and wait for the forest to grow again for a profitable harvest. That's how Georgia Pacific came to own thousands of acres on Whidbey by the mid-twentieth century.

Whidbey Island residents and environmental activists Marianne Edain and Steve Erickson explained that, as the environmental movement gained momentum in the 1970s, the federal and state government required stricter forestry and logging practices. Georgia Pacific began to divest itself of its holdings.

In 1988, the company sold some 2,500 acres of its growing forests on South Whidbey to a new real estate development company, the Trillium Corporation. Very quickly, Trillium began to clear-cut the forests it had just acquired. Public protest began with demonstrations in front of logging teams. That protest focused on protecting wetlands and streams in and next to the properties the corporation held. Edain and Erickson began investigating public records in Island County and learned that Trillium was applying for permits to clear every one of its new properties. They spread the word and protests grew, expanding from the logging sites to Island County offices and the Washington State Department of Natural Resources.

Neither government group was effective in stopping (or even slowing) the corporation's systematic clear-cuts. Local citizens continued their impassioned effort to protect the forests, its wetlands and wildlife habitat. While irritating to Trillium, the protests didn't stop the clear-cutting of many properties, including the hundreds of acres in 1988 on that ridge north of Freeland. Consistent with commercial forest practices, the corporation densely planted tree seedlings on the cleared lands. In 1997, the loggers came back for the last forty acres. Protesters again reacted vigorously but to no avail. The failure of protests to make a difference created much animosity among the residents of Whidbey for the Trillium Corporation.

In late 2000, the property was transferred to a business associate in California as the Trillium Corporation worked through bankruptcy. Some eighteen months later, the acreage was purchased by Dogwood Whidbey Development, a group of investors whose plans for a large housing development began to take shape. They proposed clusters of homes in the young forest with some single home sites on ten-acre parcels. The planned residential developments needed roads, utilities and county approval.

BENDING THE RULES

Dogwood Whidbey Development's purchase offer to acquire the eight-hundred-acre Trillium property came with at least two conditions. The first required the owners to secure approval from the Board of Island County Commissioners to move the Trillium property from its Designated Forest tax classification to Forest Open Space. This move would reduce the minimum lot size from twenty to ten acres and eliminate the requirement to pay compensating taxes for developing the property. The second condition required the owners to divide the property by unregulated segregation into eighty ten-acre lots. The owners met both of these conditions. The property was sold at a high price that clearly reflected its intended use as residential and not forestry.

For decades, the owners of the Trillium property had received a substantial tax break from the county because the property was managed for commercial forestry and not for development. Changing it to residential status should have increased taxes and initiated a process for the sellers to pay compensating taxes to account for the years when it was a forest and taxed at an extremely low rate. That's the concept behind compensating taxes—to compensate the county for lost revenue when converting property to residential development. But the county commission allowed the owners to avoid paying these back taxes when it approved moving the property into Forest Open Space.

The compensating taxes for the Trillium property would have been substantial—many hundreds of thousands of dollars. In addition, dividing the property into ten-acre lots allowed the new owners to avoid going through any kind of planning process, contrary to the spirit of the state Growth Management Act. Dogwood Whidbey and the previous two owners cleverly exploited loopholes, avoided paying compensating taxes and still created eighty residential lots.

Immediately, Dogwood cleared all forest and other vegetation from seven ten-acre lots so that potential buyers standing on those dusty and thistle-dotted lots could see from Mount Rainier to Mount Baker. They then pursued their grand plan: creating a dozen clustered residential developments totaling more than one hundred home sites they called the Estates at Whidbey. Over local protest, Island County granted preliminary approval in 2008. Dogwood Whidbey then paved roads and installed utilities at the north end of its property, a required step to go from preliminary to final approval for the development. The developers had visions of big returns on their investment.

But by the time the roads were in place, the local housing market was evaporating. Dogwood Whidbey didn't make payments on its bank loans. In October 2009, Shoreline Bank foreclosed on the property. With property values declining, the bank wanted to sell the property quickly and for the highest possible price. It was also willing to sell the property in pieces. One such sale was for eighty acres to the Freeland Water and Sewer District to be used as a repository for treated sewage water. By the close of 2009, that sale was nearing completion.

ENTER THE LAND TRUST

Reading public notices about the foreclosure, Pat Powell saw the saga unfolding. Realizing that the land wouldn't be developed immediately and that there was a chance it could remain wildlife habitat, protected watershed and community open space, she contacted the bank representative. Her initiative demonstrated what had become the land trust's professional approach to protecting some of the most important resources in Island County.

Established by a group of concerned citizens who wanted to protect the unique, natural landscape of Island County, the land trust began formally when it filed articles of incorporation with the state attorney general's office in March 1984. Like all land trusts, this one brought together a commitment to private property rights and interest in public benefit.

Land trusts work only with willing landowners who want to keep their properties intact—for whatever reason. Their principal tool is the conservation easement, a legally binding agreement that removes the development rights and often states the acceptable uses of a property. The goal is to maintain the land's conservation value forever.

Conservation easements are attached to the land and apply no matter who owns it. The land can be inherited, sold or gifted to another person, and the protections of the conservation easement remain. Only a few types of organizations, including land trusts, can hold (or own) a conservation easement. Individuals cannot. If the organization ceases to exist, for whatever reason, then the easement is transferred to another qualified organization.

When the Whidbey Camano Land Trust was founded, it received an existing conservation easement from Ebey's Landing Open Space Foundation (ELOSF) that was soon to close its operation. Over the next nineteen years, the all-volunteer land trust board worked with private property owners and protected about four hundred acres on Whidbey Island with conservation easements. By 2000, as the intense work to Save the Woods on Saratoga was coming to a close (see Chapter 12), the land trust board realized that the pressures to develop Whidbey Island were certain to increase. The island was too accessible, too popular and too beautiful to be left alone. For generations, it had been a favored place for fishing, summer vacation and quick getaways. It was becoming an increasingly preferred retirement location. So it was time to guide the land trust to the next level of professionalism to protect the unique places of Island County.

This realization translated into a commitment to raise funds to hire an executive director and open an office. The land trust hired Powell in January 2003 to lead the work of protecting the most important natural areas and farmlands in Island County. The land trust's workload was going to increase dramatically.

FOCUSED MISSION

While Dogwood Whidbey Development planned its Estates at Whidbey, the land trust was also moving forward. Powell, a planner by training and orientation, worked with the board and the local community to develop a science- and community-based plan to identify the most important areas for protection. The land trust staff reached out to private property owners in those priority areas. Over the next seven years, dozens of properties and several thousand more acres came under protection.

With each completed project, more people learned about the work of the land trust and supported its accomplishments. Parks, beaches, farmlands, forests and open space became a growing part of the resources providing public benefit. Clean water, locally grown food, wildlife habitat, quiet places, walking trails, much-loved meadows and more were permanently protected by the land trust working with property owners who loved the land and wanted future generations to enjoy it, too. The membership grew from about thirty-five households when Powell began to some eight hundred by the time the land trust celebrated its twenty-fifth anniversary.

The land trust had gained credibility, a reputation for focus on its mission and connections to the community. It was as ready as it would ever be to take on the great fundraising challenge that Powell and Cahill discussed on their way back from Shoreline Bank.

ACT OF FAITH

Key board members and staff convened an initial meeting to build a plan. They recognized that the normal process of capital campaigns couldn't apply given the times and the fundraising deadline. There was no time for quietly soliciting major gifts, followed by a very public campaign. Everything had to happen at

Aerial view of the Trillium Community Forest boundaries. *Courtesy of Whidbey Camano Land Trust.*

The campaign logo said it all. *Courtesy of the Whidbey Camano Land Trust.*

once. The land trust organized committees, each taking a major section of the campaign. They worked to create and grow community buzz, find donors at all levels and make the deal happen. They designated a campaign coordinator, created campaign materials and enlisted a small army of workers to tell the story in dozens of ways and ask for support. After only a month of preparation, the land trust went public with its ambitious goal and asked everyone who cared about land, clean water and wildlife to help.

In an act of great faith and commitment to the mission, the board voted to put all of its reserve funds toward the $4.2 million campaign goal.

The hoped-for grass-roots support materialized. An initial local newspaper article and then an e-mail announcement got the community talking. At first, small donations (fifteen to fifty dollars) came in. As the word spread, more people contributed and helped. They held house parties and other fundraisers with titles like Ride for the Forest and Dance for Trees and Memories. People painted and sang and sipped wine for the trees. Dozens wrote letters to the editor, keeping the story alive and emphasizing the urgency. People with connections contacted the media, helping secure newspaper, radio and television interviews.

Within the first two weeks, one couple donated $6,500, enough to protect one acre. Their gift made a great newspaper story that was circulated widely.

July 4 parade in Maxwelton, 2010. *Courtesy of the Whidbey Camano Land Trust.*

That generosity inspired others who offered gifts in multiples of that one-acre price. Local author Anne Linea provided a copy of her beautiful, newly published hardbound book, *Keepers of the Trees: A Guide to Re-Greening North America*, as her thank-you gift for anyone who saved an acre. Up and down the island, dozens of people asked friends and colleagues to donate. Some local groups established match challenges to encourage people to donate. Small collection boxes placed in thirty retail outlets became mini-billboards for the movement. Teen equestrians went door-to-door telling the story and asking for donations. Local businesses designated Save the Forest events and donated all proceeds from various sales.

Donations and pledges came in—first a trickle and then many each day. Several people bought lottery tickets, hoping to win big and buy the forest. The June deadline approached. The land trust had raised a third of the money and secured a back-up loan for another 25 percent of the purchase price. But they were still far from the goal and the banks were increasingly anxious to sell the property. Powell negotiated a three-month extension.

THE GAME CHANGER

Initially euphoric with the extension, the Whidbey community and the land trust were exhausted and uncertain about what else to do. The campaign lost some momentum, but efforts continued. A land trust staff member made a successful contact with a journalism intern, Carly Flandro of the *Seattle Times*. Flandro's front-page feature story on August 3, 2010, opened a new chapter in the campaign.

Calls came that morning from across Puget Sound. People with no direct connection to Whidbey Island sent money to help. The giving coordinators of major philanthropists made inquiries. As the word spread through the Internet, donations flooded in from across the country, even from other countries. Some people sent notes with their checks or online donations. They wrote about needing to care for nature, about wanting to be part of an effort to protect land and forests and care for wildlife. Many shared how much they loved Whidbey Island and the wonderful memories of visits or growing up here.

The largest single donor had no real connection to Whidbey Island but was deeply concerned about the many effects of deforestation. As part of the initial vetting of the project's worthiness, her representative asked two questions: "Was the community behind this effort? Was the land trust putting its own money into the campaign?" The answer to both was a resounding YES!

LAST-MINUTE DRAMA

Gifts continued to come in. At the property, the tree-shaped thermometer showing donations was updated weekly. Local newspapers reported regularly how things were going. The increased fundraising reduced the amount needed in the loan. Every day was both exciting and anxious. Still no one knew for sure whether there would be enough money to save the forest.

Stock donations, including those sold on international markets, created some hiccups as the days sped toward the deadline. One of the banks in the consortium was taken over by the Federal Deposit Insurance Corporation. Pressure mounted from the two remaining banks to close sooner or risk a huge penalty. Checks didn't arrive as donors had promised and had to be tracked down. Staff contacted several hundred people to fulfill their pledges.

Powell resolved some title issues on the parcels and renegotiated with adjacent landowners on a roadway easement.

Finally, after seven months of intense effort, money was in escrow, and the documents all signed. The pieces seemed to be in place for closing on September 29, 2010. If anything delayed the final transaction, there would be no extension.

With so much at stake, Powell spent much of the afternoon of September 29 at the Island County offices shepherding the transaction through its final stage. Each of the fifty-five parcels needed to be recorded separately to ensure accurate title transfer. The county's new computer system stumbled several times in the process. At 3:55 p.m., five minutes before the computer would automatically shut down for the weekend, the final parcel was recorded.

The deal was done. The race had been won. Staff and board (and their spouses and partners) raised glasses in joyful, weary celebration.

What's in a Name

Almost immediately, people began to ask what the forest would be called. Popularly, the land was known as the Trillium Woods, but for some, the name carried much bitterness. The land trust asked the community for nominations and received ninety-five suggestions—diverse, playful, serious, thoughtful. A committee was assembled to review the names and, with explanation, recommend a choice to the board.

Trillium Community Forest. Controversial, yes, but it represented the uniqueness of the woods, the challenges of keeping it "rooted" and well-tended so it would flourish and its simple beauty. Trilliums could grow there, and the name is part of the story. The name "embodies what happened here. It's more than the past. It's also what it means to all of us now."

Community means people working together. The community saved the forest and will care for it long into the future. The word *community* acknowledges that this forest is for both people and wildlife for many generations to come. It is a forest, a huge, uninterrupted expanse of trees and wildlife habitat. It is not a woods.

The name reflects "what we did together." It tells the great story of the property, the ownership, the history and the many people involved.

GROWING GRASS ROOTS

An idea—daring and unlikely, yet promoting the general welfare. A few people believe, and their enthusiasm catches on. Lots of hard work builds momentum. The community around it grows and grows. The unlikely happens, and new ideas bubble up.

To develop the Public Use Plan for the area, the land trust actively sought input from community groups and scientists. The final plan embodies the premise that all groups need to share this wonderful resource. No single group deserves more than any other. Even those without a voice, like wildlife, need to be considered. It's their forest, too. Learning to share and respect other's needs is an opportunity for personal and community growth.

This dramatic history is the story of people working together in difficult times to accomplish a great end. Now the story needs to shift—people working together, fostering respect for nature and one another. The community saved the forest; now the forest can build community.

14
The Three Sisters Family Farm

For five generations, the Muzzall family has nurtured its farm and one another. The growth of industrial farming challenges the viability of family farms and, for many years, reduced their numbers. Hard work, careful management and a passion for farming keeps the Three Sisters Family Farm vibrant and its high-quality grass-fed beef available for the local market and beyond. Love of the land and a commitment to future generations led the family to develop a conservation easement of its land.

JENNIFER MUZZALL-JONES'S EYES light up as she describes the cattle, chickens and hogs she raises on the Three Sisters Family Farm. Nearby fields of premium grass, dotted by stands of evergreen trees and wetlands, stretch north from an array of farm buildings. Some of the older, wooden structures were built in previous decades by past generations of the Muzzall family. The lush land is home to an array of wildlife, including at least nine different raptor species. To the south, just across the road, the waters of Penn Cove lap the beach below the bluff where the family home sits on the site of the original farmhouse.

Jennifer is the eldest of the three sisters for whom the farm is named. Ron and Shelly Muzzall, her parents, say she is the "animal" person in the family. As she talks, her arms cradle a large and contented cat. Plump Black Angus steers graze in the nearby pasture. Sounds of 350 laying hens drift through the air.

"Community is important," Jennifer said. "In addition to using our own land, I lease pasture from my neighbors. In return I take good care of it and produce something that people want. We all pull together to make things work."

Above: This centennial farm overlooks Penn Cove. Across the water lies Coupeville, the oldest town in Washington and once home to three villages of Lower Skagit tribal people. *Courtesy of the Muzzall family*.

Left: "Running a farm isn't just for boys," say the three Muzzall sisters, Jessica, Roshel and Jennifer. *Courtesy of the Muzzall family.*

She points out historic Coupeville, just across the water. "When my great-grandparents first came, it was a permanent home site for the Native Americans who lived on Whidbey Island. They used to come here for the potatoes my great-grandparents grew."

Jessica, the middle sister, is equally as excited as she talks about the new Three Sisters Farm Store that she manages in nearby San de Fuca. Featured are eggs from their hens, hot dogs, sausage and steaks, along with other "Made on Whidbey" products such as Hunter's Moon Blueberry Farm honey and sauces, Bell's Farm berries, Screaming Banshee breads, Island Trollers wild caught albacore and Willowood Farm vegetables.

Jessica describes how she does direct marketing. She lets the farm's devoted following know when new products arrive via Facebook posts and e-mail. "The goods fly off the shelf. People stop here all day long," she reported. She actively seeks out new vendors who sell good quality products that customers have requested.

Roshel, the youngest Muzzall sister, is honing her skills at Bellevue College while she considers the role she might want to take in the family business. In the meantime she helps out at the farm store.

THROUGH THE GENERATIONS

Three Sisters Family Farm is more than a name; it is a legacy of five generations of hard work and love of the land. The first Muzzalls, Edwin and Stella, came by train from the Midwest in the late 1800s. They arrived on Whidbey Island the only way possible—by steamboat. When they purchased the property in what is now Ebey's Reserve, overlooking Penn Cove, there were few roads. When they went to town for supplies, it was by canoe.

The land was heavily forested. Edwin and Stella planted potatoes and other crops along the banks of Penn Cove in a garden where the trees had already been burned off. That's how the Lower Skagit tribes that preceded them created planting areas. Anything they produced for sale traveled to Langley and other local markets by boat. Unfortunately Edwin died at a young age. Stella remained on the farm, living in the family home on the bluff.

Lyle, Edwin and Stella's son, began clearing the land in 1910 for what would become a two-hundred-acre family farm, later growing to six hundred acres with the addition of leased land. It was back-breaking work. Huge trees had to be cut and the land cleared of stumps. He tackled it one acre at a time. By 1920, dairy cattle were grazing on hard-won pastureland.

Lyle Muzzall began clearing land at a time when family farming had reached a pinnacle in the United States. There were 6.4 million farms nationwide, most of them small but able to support the families that lived on them. Within a few short years mechanized farm tools, such as the combine harvester, began to push small farms out. To afford the new technology, farms needed to be bigger. By 1950, many small farms had been absorbed by bigger, often corporate-owned operations. Others were lost to development of one type or another. The total number of farms in the country had dropped to 5.6 million. Some families had to take non-farm jobs to stay on their farm.

FARMING ON WHIDBEY ISLAND

Whidbey Island is surrounded by the temperate waters of Puget Sound and blessed with moist, mild winters and long hours of summer sunlight. The quality of the soils coupled with a moderate climate makes it possible to raise a wide variety of fruits, vegetables, livestock and flowers.

While the trend toward large, corporate-owned farms was occurring in other parts of the country, farms on Whidbey Island remained relatively small and family owned. The island isn't able to support commodity agriculture—the big industrial farms that often specialize in one major crop such as corn or soybeans.

In 1935, about 850 farms operated on Whidbey Island. Many of them had large strawberry fields. Farmers also grew vegetables and other types of fruits and berries and raised chickens and beef cattle. A cannery had been built in Oak Harbor in 1910 to process all the berries, and an egg cooperative was organized in 1912. Later, a large commercial cannery was built in Langley that supplied the Puget Sound region with canned fruits and vegetables. Only six farms were larger than five hundred acres in size, including those owned by the Muzzalls and the Sherman family.

Roger Sherman, whose family also began farming on Whidbey in the late 1800s, describes the phases of agriculture on Whidbey Island. He says grains, and particularly wheat, were important crops. Wheat grows really well on Whidbey. It's a cool-season grass that likes long, mild days and lots of water. By the 1930s, Whidbey Island held the world record for wheat production. Farmers on Ebey's Prairie grew up to 119 bushels of wheat per acre.

Sherman tells how potatoes became a popular crop and talks about the Chinese immigrants who worked the potato fields. They were eventually forced, because of discrimination, to leave. In the 1940s, turkeys became popular, and a large turkey processing plant was built in Oak Harbor. Dairy farming had become an important business by then, and dairies were located from South to North Whidbey. The Shermans and the Muzzalls had large dairy herds.

Whidbey Island produce and dairy products used to go to grocery stores and food cooperatives throughout Puget Sound. But as agriculture grew more corporate and grocery stores evolved into big box stores with ever-lower prices, Whidbey farms couldn't compete. Many farms went out of business, and the land was sold for development. The last dairy farm, owned by the Shermans, stopped operation in 2008.

Today, farming on Whidbey Island reflects changes occurring across the country. After decades of decline, the number of family farms is growing again. The island is home to an increasing number of small, organic operations, many of them owned or leased by young people. Quite a few rely on non-farm income to supplement what they earn from farming. These small, niche farms produce an array of high-quality specialty products, from fruits and vegetables to flowers, meats, cheeses, fresh eggs, soaps and other hand-crafted items.

These new farmers engage in an approach gaining popularity: direct-to-consumer marketing. The farmers sell at farmers' markets, from their own farm stands and U-pick fields, through community-shared agriculture (CSA) agreements, on the Internet and to restaurants and other retail business. While it is still a small percentage of overall farm revenue, direct-to-consumer marketing of food products now generates more than $1 billion a year in sales nationally and is growing.

THE THREE SISTERS FARM

"I always knew I wanted to farm," Ron Muzzall said. He and Shelly met and married in college; they graduated, and Ron returned to Whidbey Island with Shelly in 1986. Ron began farming with his dad, Bob Muzzall. Dairy farming had by then become a large-scale business. Industrial farms in other parts of the country ran herds that ran in the thousands.

To keep up, the Muzzalls needed to increase the size of their dairy herd. After careful consideration, Ron invested in Jersey cows and, over time, expanded from fifty to two hundred animals. Shelly took a major role in caring for the cows and kept track of their production. "We worked all the time—all of us," Shelly said. "Our kids grew up knowing that you had to work in life."

By 2006, the Muzzalls' farm was one of only two dairy farms left on the island. In 1985, there had been ten. "When my dad and my granddad started farming, if you worked hard enough you could get ahead," Ron said. "With technology and mechanization growing so fast, farming became a lot riskier, and making a living was a lot harder. I looked ahead and realized we couldn't keep up with the dairy business. Fortunately, I bought the right breed of cows; the price of Jerseys went up when we decided to sell. It was the right time. Milk and cow prices dropped the week after we sold our herd."

The Muzzalls faced a tough decision: sell out completely and move on or figure out another way to make a go of it. It was more than an economic decision; it was about their family legacy. Four generations of Muzzalls had lived on and worked the land; a fifth generation was growing up in the same tradition. Every morning, from the time they were little, Jennifer, Jessica and Roshel got up, met their grandparents at the driveway that separated their two houses and went with them to help feed the calves. Farming was the life they knew.

Ron and Shelly began to think about another type of farming, one that capitalized on the popularity of the high-quality grass-fed beef for which they were already known. For several years, under the name Three Sisters Cattle Company, the family had been raising grass-fed beef and selling it locally as a side business. They created the company, in part, to give their daughters an opportunity to earn money for college and learn the family business. They marketed their beef primarily through local farmers markets, their own farm stand and the Internet.

Ron and Shelly decided they had a good product and a compelling story to tell. Successful family farm owners like the Muzzalls pursue a fundamentally different approach to farming than do corporate farmers. Because they have a passion for what they do, they do it better. They focus on what they do best and substitute hard work and frugal management for capital investment.

The Muzzalls decided to expand the direct-to-consumer marketing approach they had already developed. Their customers are their community.

The Muzzall family (left to right): Roshel; Jessica; Shelly; Ron; son-in law, Tom; and Jennifer. *Courtesy of the Muzzall family.*

The customer knows them and their product. They know what customers want. Farms that market through large distributors pay up to eighty cents of each dollar for processing, transportation, packaging, advertising and other marketing services. By cutting out the middleman and selling directly to the customer, the Muzzalls keep more of their revenue and are better able to reinvest in their farm and community.

Now the Muzzalls raise grass and produce high-quality grass-fed beef. That's their primary business. They are the largest commercial cattle operation on Whidbey Island, and Three Sisters Cattle Company has become the Three Sisters Family Farm.

In addition to beef, the Muzzalls sell pork, turkey, chicken and cage-free eggs directly to seven island groceries, a handful of restaurants and, of course, through their own local store. Off-island, their hot dogs and pepperoni sticks are marketed to outlets throughout Puget Sound, including the Seattle School District and as far away as Southeast Alaska.

Their timing was good. Mad cow disease got people's attention. They began to look more closely at where and how beef was grown and processed. Awareness of food safety issues began to grow. Many people, along with businesses, schools and other organizations, figured out that a lower ticket price on food wasn't always a good value. They began to buy locally through

Overlooking Penn Cove, even the pigs have a great view. *Courtesy of the Muzzall family.*

farmers' markets, food coops, U-picks, farm stands and the Internet. Now a growing number of people are willing to pay a little more for good food.

The family continues to develop innovative ways to market locally. As Jennifer explained, it's all about community. Their customers know them and trust the quality of their products. Jessica came up with the idea of a limited seasonal farmers' market in the Muzzall barn on the third Saturday of October, November and December. Other farmers' markets on the island close up by October, so there hasn't been a place to bring late season crops. More than ten Whidbey Island farms now participate.

FOR THE NEXT GENERATION

The Golden Rule of sustainable farming is to meet present needs while leaving equal or better opportunities for farmers in the future and supporting the local community. That means two things for the Muzzalls: farming in a way that is both economically viable and ecologically sound and making sure the land is protected for future generations.

Their website (http://www.3sistersbeef.com) describes how they accomplish sustainability: "It is really just a way of life from what we eat to how we heat our home. This has really not changed for many generations. The biggest problem on any farm is really just cash, from generating it to keeping it. So conserving is a way of life, from used wire to used equipment."

The family plants primarily alfalfa and grass or clover and grass. The complement of legumes and grass provide for each other. Pesticides and commercial fertilizers cost money. The Muzzalls use the manure from the animals for fertilizer. It doesn't require cash and its better for the environment. The carbon sequestration rate is high on their farm because 95 percent of the land is sod or timber. They use an integrated pest management system that relies on a combination of common-sense practices based on understanding the life cycles of pests and their interaction with the environment. Pesticides are used sparingly, primarily to control weeds in the fencerows and where the timber and agriculture lands meet.

On July 17, 2010, the Muzzalls celebrated four generations and a century of farming. As in any small business, keeping the farm going from one generation to another is a major challenge. If a farm or ranch family has not adequately planned for succession, its operation is likely to go out of business, be absorbed into ever-larger farming neighbors or be used for development.

About 70 percent of U.S. farmland will change hands in the next twenty years, but many family operations do not have a next generation skilled in or willing to continue farming. This isn't a problem in the Muzzall family. The three daughters have already begun to take on major roles in the farm's management. That is consistent with a trend that suggests that, within the next twenty years, the majority of farmland in the United States will be owned by women. It is thought by many that as women, like the Muzzall sisters, become farm owners, they will be more likely to employ conservation practices.

Ron notes the important role that strong Muzzall women have taken throughout the history of the farm, starting with his great-grandmother Stella and continuing through the years to his wife and daughters. He points

Aerial view of the Three Sisters Family Farm, overlooking Penn Cove, including land protected by the Whidbey Camano Land Trust. *Courtesy of Whidbey Camano Land Trust and photographer Greg Ridder.*

out that each generation of women nurtured the next, took care of their own families and worked beside their husbands to keep the farm viable.

Ron and Shelly want to make sure the land is available to their daughters as well as future generations. That's what led them to permanently place 113 pristine acres—the part of the farm that is the hub of their operation—into a conservation easement. They worked with the Whidbey Camano Land Trust to guarantee that their land will be available for farming forever.

The land trust obtained funds from the Island County Conservation Futures Fund and federal and state grants to purchase the development rights from the Muzzalls as part of the conservation easement process. A conservation easement makes it easier to pass the farm on to the next generation.

BUILDING LEGACIES A DAY AT A TIME

The world has certainly changed since Lyle Muzzall began cutting trees and digging out stumps to create farmland. But the pioneering spirit of Edwin and Stella has carried the family through challenge and change. It continues as Ron and Shelly prepare their daughters for a new world of farming.

Across Penn Cove, the lights of Coupeville begin to twinkle as night falls. Jessica and Jennifer each stop by their parents' home before they head to their own homes. The legacy is passed on at the kitchen table, just as it was done in previous generations. The family talks about the day, shares stories about the past and makes plans for the future.

The Dance Goes On

As we look at the evolving history of Whidbey Island, it is important to remember that environmental consciousness, including concepts such as sustainability and species interdependency, were not widely accepted until the early 1970s. Although Rachel Carson's book *The Silent Spring* was published in 1962 and is credited with starting the environmental movement in the United States, it was not until the social and political upheaval of the early '70s that popular attention began to focus on these issues.

Until then, people simply did not have a framework to discern what was at stake or the language to talk about it clearly. Although they were distressed and angry about insults to their environment, without a common vocabulary their response was formless. They were thus propelled into public arenas where definitions, science, regulations, case law and mitigation techniques were developed from the mix of conflict and compromise occurring in the growing environmental movement.

We have learned a lot during the past four decades. We know that people and the land are intimate partners in a continuing story. Look at one, and you will know much about the other. Just as in any relationship, each influences and responds to the other as participants in a tangible connection and shared history.

The land gives evidence of the spiritual, cultural, economic, social and political patterns of people who have lived on it over time. A close look tells us whether the land has nurtured community or conflict and whether this interaction has enlivened or dispirited individuals. Most often the relationship is a quiet dance of action and reaction. Human action engenders response within the environment. People then adjust and respond to these changes, and the dance goes on.

The connection between people and the land can be better understood by examining iterations at play in all human relationships. Over centuries and cultures, people have demonstrated both respect and understanding for their environment as well as rapacious domination and control. Some have seen the land as something to be deeply understood and honored, others as something to be harshly mastered and heedlessly degraded. Many people behave as though the land is simply painted background scenery for their acquisitive dreams and busy lives, and that indifference takes its own toll.

GROWING WILLINGNESS TO ACT

Interspersed in quiet, commonplace activities and life-cycle changes are instances of high drama, as when landscape is permanently altered by human hands or when people face the consequences of cataclysmic natural events. Part of this unfolding series of events is the cultural life cycle of human beings: elders teaching children, values being instilled, remembrance of wisdom and traditions.

The special places on Whidbey Island that we visit in this book illustrate all these themes. Most of the lands we describe were changed forever as people harvested old-growth forest and prioritized agricultural activities. Dikes, dredging and development further altered the landscape. Always, the land is in various states of recovery or adaptation based on human choices.

In some heartening examples like the Trillium Community Forest, people stepped forward to stop planned environmental damage and begin painstaking restoration. In a very few, such as Deception Pass State Park and South Whidbey State Park, areas were saved in their relatively pristine states from irreparable damage.

Some places were altered over time by economic decisions but then repurposed. Bayview, the Whidbey Institute and Three Sisters Farm are examples of places where people took new interest in place, repaired where possible and moved into a new mode of stewardship based on carefully articulated values and goals to nurture community.

Despite clear progress, the environmental movement itself is not immune to conflict. There have always been strong points of view about how best to respond to environmental threats. Should open land be left just as is? How do we balance needs for housing and employment with their effects on the environment? Even efforts to restore and repair land are not without conflict. Is it OK to remove invasive plants? What about bringing in native plants? How can we manage the needs of competing species?

We operate in a far from perfect world and are constantly challenged to work together in new ways to make progress. Environmental protection at Double Bluff, Greenbank Farm and Ebey's Landing National Historical Reserve is the result of hours of volunteer time and tremendous creativity. People worked hard to find reasons things could work, rather than focusing on the many reasons they could fail. In other instances of community dialogue, we learned that collaboration can be messy and unsatisfying when those involved hold uncompromising positions that place land before people or economic development before land.

Our growing knowledge in environmental issues has enabled us collectively to see more clearly, to understand more complexity and to act more consciously. More people share a basic understanding about how their actions affect the land and appreciate the benefit in protecting our shared environment. They are ready to do their part.

Thankfully, we have a growing willingness to act, but crucial questions remain. Do we have enough time to stop destructive processes already begun? In the case of Baby Island, the tidal action related to residential development will probably destroy the shrinking island completely within a few years. In the Trillium Community Forest, restoration efforts are at work to mitigate the destructive scraping of a few decades ago. How the woods will look in twenty years is not known, nor is the community's use and care of the woods without controversy.

WATCH AND HOPE

Will our growing scientific knowledge come quickly enough to offer desperately needed solutions? Will new fisheries or agricultural practices emerge that can enable third-generation pioneer families in Maxwelton Valley to prosper on their farms and also accommodate salmon so that they can return and thrive in their accustomed watershed habitat? So far, despite diligent attention and a variety of strategies intended to reinvigorate salmon runs, the fish have not returned in any significant numbers.

Like people, this heron relies on a healthy environment. *Courtesy of Whidbey Camano Land Trust and photographer Mark Sheehan.*

EPILOGUE

How can a community balance a complicated picture like the one that exists in Dugualla Bay? Land and habitat restoration, deep political divisions and national defense priorities add complexity to the mix there. Can research, new technology and community compromise come in time? We take steps, we watch and we hope.

Many of us strive to reach political consensus on the balance between private property rights and a healthy environment. The residents of Lagoon Point are committed to restoring eelgrass because it creates a healthy fish habitat, but the saltwater marsh in which eelgrass had thrived was dredged years ago for the construction of homes. That rich habitat is not recoverable. Lagoon Point and many other areas on Whidbey Island illustrate variations of the theme that what's done is done, what's gone is gone and now what? What are realistic goals given our knowledge, personal priorities and political will? How can we move from valuing instant gratification and accepting exploitation of both land and people to a longer view of generosity, health and respect for our limited natural resources?

We must develop a new way of thinking that values environmental health and community vigor as much as short-term economic benefit. The "green" restoration at Bayview Corner was far more costly than a strip mall would have been, but the benefits to people are clear at every street dance and farmers' market. People park there on expensive grass-grid parking lots, and because they do, there is less toxic run-off and coastal water quality improves incrementally. How can we build on this and provide incentives to encourage others to protect the environment?

On Whidbey Island, this very small and beloved place, we are trying to answer these questions. We are sisters and brothers of those in every community who are determined to save our earth's special places and to build healthy futures for people and creatures of this beautiful planet.

Index

About the Authors

Like many before them, Elizabeth Guss, Mary Richardson and Janice O'Mahony came to Whidbey Island and fell in love with the place. From backgrounds in business, higher education and public policy, they are now active in the community and nonprofit culture that is part of Whidbey Island's sense of place. Strong supporters of land protection, they love writing and storytelling.

Courtesy Bob Kulwin.